WILD SWIMMING Walks

WEST WALES
28 coast, river & waterfall
days out

Nia Lloyd Knott

WILD swimming

Walks

Aberystw
Aberaeron
18
17
16
Cardigan
15
14
Lampet
Newcastle
Emlyn
28
13
12
Fishguard
11
10
27
St Davids
8
9
5
Carmarthen
Llan
Haverfordwest
Whitland
St. Clears
Narberth
7
Laugharne
6
Milford
Haven
Cydweli
Saunderfoot
4
1
Pembroke
Burry
Port
Llanelli
Tenby
3
2

20

21
22
23
24

25

26
Machynlleth
Llanwrtyd Wells
Llandovery
rynaman
Glyn-neath
'ontardawe
Neath
'nsea
Port Talbot

THE WALKS

TABLE OF WALKS

No.	NAME	SWIMMING
1	Tenby's Wilder Side	Sea at Monkstone, Waterwynch, North Beach, Harbour Steps, Castle Beach and South Beach
2	Skrinkle and Manorbier	Sea at Church Doors Cove, Swanlake Bay, Manorbier and Presipe
3	Stackpole	Sea near Trefalen Farm Campsite, Broadhaven South, Stackpole Quay and Barafundle Bay
4	Angle Peninsula	Sea at Freshwater west, West Pickard Bay and West Angle Bay
5	Llawhaden	Pools in the Eastern Cleddau river
6	Dale Peninsula	Sea at Dale Harbour, sandy beaches at Castlebeach Bay, Watwick Bay, Mill Bay and West Dale Bay
7	Marloes Peninsula	Sandy and rocky beaches at Marloes Sands, Martin's Haven and Musselwick Sands
8	Solva	Sea at Solva Harbour, sandy beaches at Porthmynawyd and Porth Gwadn
9	St Non's and St Davids	Sea at St Non's Bay, harbour at Porthclais, tidal pools and coasteering at Ogof Golchfa, sandy beach at Porthlly
10	Carn Llidi and St Davids Head	Three sandy beaches - Whitesands, Porthlleuog and Porthmelgan
11	Abereiddy and Trefin	Sandy beach and flooded quarry pool at Abereiddy, sandy beach at Traeth Llyfn and rocky cove at Trefin.
12	Abermawr	Beaches at Aberbach, Abermawr and Pwllstrodur. Deep open water swim off point at Penmorfa.
13	Dinas Island	Sandy beaches at Pwllgwaelod and Cwm yr Eglwys, with options for longer swims and coasteering to explore further coves.
14	Moylgrove	Rocky cove at Ceibwr Bay, channel at mouth of Ceibwr bay, tidal pool and cave at Pwll y Wrach.
15	Teifi Gorge at Cilgerran	Shorter river dips in the Teifi or one long swim down the gorge.
16	Aberporth and Mwnt	Sea swims from sandy beaches at Aberporth and Mwnt. Challenging access to remote tidal cove at Traeth Gwy
17	Llangrannog and Penbryn	Sea swims from sandy beaches at Llangrannog and Penbryn. Challenging access to sandy cove at Traeth Bach.
18	Cwmtydu	Sea swims at rocky coves in Cwmtydu, Traeth Soden, and Castell Bach. Waterfall showers and dips at Nanterr
19	Aberystwyth to Borth Train Walk	Sea swims on sand and stone beaches at Aberystwyth South Beach, Aberystwyth North Beach, Clarach Bay, V and Borth.
20	Cwm Einion	Deep waterfall pool at Dyfi Furnace and river pool with cascade in Cwm Einion
21	Dyffryn Castell and Llynnoed Ieuan	Lake swims at Llynnoed Ieuan
22	Cwm Rheidol	River swims in Afon Rheidol
23	Pontarfynach	River swims in Afon Mynach
24	Teifi Pools and Claerddu	Waterfall dip at Claerddu and Lake swims at Llyn Fyrddon Fach and Fyrddon Fawr
25	Drygarn Fawr	Pools and waterfall in the Afon Gwesyn, and pools and gorge in the Afon Irfon
26	Doethie Valley and Llyn Brianne	Pool at the confluence of the Afon Doethie and Afon Tywi, pool and section of gorge in the Doethie
27	Abergorlech	Dipping pools in the Afon Gorlech and section of deep gorge in the Cothi
28	Henllan Circular	Large pool and narrow gorge in the Afon Teifi

RAIN	REFRESHMENTS EN ROUTE	MILES	DIFFICULTY
t path with several very steep climbs, some lane walking and woodland paths	Trevayne Farm Shop, huge selection in Tenby, Street Kitchen Kiosk New Hedges	4.0	Medium
t path with several very steep climbs, some lane walking and fields	YHA Skrinkle Café, Castle Inn Manorbier, Manorbier Castle Tea Rooms	4.0	Medium
, sand and muddy paths. Steep steps and one steep climb down on rocks.	National Trust Boathouse Café at Stackpole Quay	5.0	Medium
dunes, undulating coast path with lots of steep climbs, some lane walking	Wavecrest Café at Angle, Old Point House Pub East Angle	3.0	Easy
dland tracks, fields and some lane walking	None	5.5	Hard
t path with a few steep slopes and steps, fields and lane walking	The Griffin Inn and Boathouse Café, Dale	3.0	Easy
t path, fields, slopes and steps, steep climb down to Musselwick Sands	Runwayskiln Café and Lockley Lodge	3.5	Easy
h coast path, steep climbs, fields and a couple of stiles	Harbour Inn, Ship Inn, Cambrian Inn, 35 Main Street, Café on the Quay, all in Solva	3.5	Hard
y coast path with steps and slopes, very steep climb down and rock nbling to access the swims at St Non's and Ogof Golchfa. Some lane walking.	Porthclais Kiosk, wide range of option in St Davids	8.0	Hard
y coast path with steps and slopes. Scramble down to Porthlleuog. Short scramble to get to top of Carn Llidi.	Whitesands Beach House café	1.5	Easy
h coast path with several steep climbs and steps. Walking through fields short lane section.	The Sloop Inn and The Shed, Porthgain	3.0	Medium
dland paths and farm tracks, good coast path with some steep climbs, some ng on quiet lanes. Steep climb down and rock scramble to water at Penmorfa.	Café at Melin Tregwynt	5.0	Hard
trodden path with steep climbs and descents, steps and slopes.Flat path een the two beaches.	Sailor's Safety pub at Pwllgwaelod	4.5	Medium
dland paths, coast path with steep climbs, farm track and lane walking	None	5.5	Hard
, muddy woodland paths and lanes	Siop y Pentre, Cilgerran and Glasshouse Café, Welsh Wildlife Centre	5.5	Hard
dland paths, fields, lanes and coast path. Steps and steep climbs, with one steep climb down to Traeth Gwyrddon	Caban Mwnt kiosk, several options at Aberporth	6.5	Hard
dland paths, steep coast path, fields, lanes and tracks, all of which can me muddy. Steep rocky scramble down to Traeth Bach.	Plwmp Tart Tea rooms, Penbryn. Pentre Arms, Beach Hut and Tafell a Tân in Llangrannog	7.5	Hard
dland paths, steep slopes, muddy fields, lane walking, coast path and steep	None	5.5	Hard
steep climbs on good coast path, rocky and muddy in places. Some ng on pavements through the towns.	Try Baravin, Victoria Inn and Uncle Alberts. Refereshments at Clarach Bay Caravan Park	3.5	Easy
st tracks and lane walking, some muddy and overgrown sections	None	2.0	Easy
d track for first and last part of walk, very steep climb and some very y and tussocky terrain.	None	6.0	Hard
dland paths, some steep climbs, farmland tracks, can be very muddy. Small on of lane walking.	Statkraft Café, Cwm Rheidol	6.0	Medium
tracks, woodland paths, forestry tracks, small section of boggy ground and tion of lane walking	The Hafod Hotel, Pontarfynach	7.5	Medium
tracks, boggy ground, pathless tussocky terrain, lane and muddy and stony	None	3.0	Medium
and tracks, boggy, and tussocky trackless terrain, and long section of lane	None	3.5	Easy
s, boggy and muddy paths, steep climb, forestry tracks	None	3.5	Easy
stry tracks, very short section of lane, and muddy woodland path	Y Llew Du pub, Abergorlech	4.0	Medium
s, fields, muddy woodland paths and marshy fields	The Leeky Barrel, Henllan	7.0	Medium

Sunset at Mwnt beach

INTRODUCTION

If you dream of emerald seas, wild-flower-jewelled clifftops, quiet coves, tales of saints and sailors, princes and poets, ruined castles and abandoned mines, remote moorland lakes and deep river valleys, then you have come to the right place. West Wales has all of the above to discover, whether you're walking the coast path on a sunny summer's day, or drinking up the solitude in its hinterlands.

This book has been a long time in the making. A lifetime in fact. Having grown up next door in South Wales, our family took regular trips to the coast of Pembrokeshire, where my parents would drag my brother, my sister and me out to walk the coast path around St Davids, Forthgain and Strumble Head. We were pretty unenthusiastic, as most teenagers tend to be about walking for pleasure, but clearly these early trips ignited something in me, as I continued to return again and again as an adult, feeling an intangible draw to the western coasts, hills and valleys of my homeland.

I've walked most of the Pembrokeshire and Ceredigion coastline, some parts many, many times, and I've got to know the extent of the Elenydd upland region, otherwise known as the Cambrian Mountains. For the past eight years through my work as a guide with my business Wild Trails Wales, I've helped others to discover West Wales, sharing its scenery, history, wildlife and culture with guests from more than 50 countries, and organised nature connection experiences for those living locally.

Working on this book was a dream project. Doing justice to such a special corner of the world was always going to be a big challenge, and I've felt the weight of making sure each of the walks in this book allows you to experience the very best of this area. I've waded through miles of mud, thigh-deep bog and heather, persisted through two of the wettest summers in recent records, consistently covered in bruises and bramble scratches, and sat down and cried with exhaustion, or through defeat when my planned route didn't work out, so you don't have to.

Broadhaven South

But more importantly, I have basked in crystal waters under cloudless skies, explored caves, sunbathed in quiet coves, smiled at seals that popped up to eyeball me from the water, come face to face with a metre-long snake, gasped as a peregrine falcon snatched a pigeon out of the air only metres away from where I was standing, feasted on wild berries, skinny-dipped in sparkling mountain streams, leapt from rocks, swam at sunset and watched the full moon rise while eating chips at the beach with good friends. I need not have worried. West Wales is simply so magical that it sells itself.

St David's Head

On each and every walk you'll find spectacular scenery, wonderful wildlife, beautiful places to swim, fascinating history and a rich culture that I believe can match anywhere in the world. I hope, if you're a visitor, that you'll fall as deeply in love with this land as I have, and continue to return again and again. And if you're lucky enough to live here, I hope that you can find something new to inspire you amongst these pages, and that it matches up to the pride that you no doubt feel here, 'Adre' – Home.

THE WILD WEST

Those who didn't know are often amazed to find out how wonderful West Wales is for nature and wildlife. The amazing flora, fauna, geology and of course the water of the west are part of the reason I love it so much and, more than being just an excellent playground for adventures, this is what makes it truly special. I've included as much information about the wildlife of each location as possible in each chapter. Through the walks in this book alone you'll visit ten Special Areas of Conservation, more than twenty Sites of Special Scientific Interest, a Marine Conservation Zone, a National Park and an UNESCO Biosphere. There is a vast range of special habitats, and they all provide homes for different kinds of wildlife, plants, and undertake different roles in the environment.

The most obvious is the coastal environment, the prominent feature of this book. The coast holds a variety of specialised habitats such as offshore islands near Marloes Peninsula (Walk 7) and Carn Llidi and St Davids Head (10), kelp beds, particularly around St Non's and St Davids (Walk 9), Abereiddy and Trefin (Walk 11), and Marloes Peninsula (7), and rare and threatened sea grass meadows on Dale Peninsula (Walk 6) and Angle Peninsula (4).

Wetlands are important, particularly for birds and aquatic species such as otters. Explore these on or near the walks at Cwm Einion (Walk 20), Abermawr (12), Teifi Gorge (15, Dale Peninsula (6) and at Cors Caron near the Teifi Pools (24).

The hills and valleys also hold unique and special environments. Fragments of rare Celtic Rainforest, particularly rich in plant species, can be found near Llyn Brianne (Walk 26), and in Cwm Einion (20) and Cwm Rheidol (22). Peatlands and mire, or bog, are hugely important for carbon storage and water regulation. These can be found in the uplands of the Elenydd region of this book at Drygarn Fawr (Walk 25), Dyffryn Castell and Llynnoed Ieuan (21) and the Teifi Pools (24). The sense of space, peace and solitude in these areas is unrivalled.

So, what wildlife might you find in these special habitats? The coast of West Wales is host to a wide range of cetaceans (whales, dolphins and porpoises). Cardigan Bay supports the UK's only resident population of bottlenose dolphins – between two and three hundred of them call the West Wales coast home. One of the best places to see them from land is at Mwnt on walk 16. Other species of dolphin and harbour porpoises can be seen all along the coast; some of my favourite places to spot them are St Davids Head (Walk 10) and on the Marloes Peninsula (7). A good tip for spotting them from land is to see if there are any birds, particularly gannets, circling. Below them, you may well spot cetaceans feeding.

East Blockhouse, Angle Peninsula

Abereiddy Blue Lagoon

Musselwick

Porthclais

Dawn swim at Solva

The coast is also an important breeding ground for Atlantic Grey Seals, with large colonies around Skomer and Ramsey Island just offshore from St Davids Head (Walk 10) and the Marloes Peninsula (7), and can often be seen particularly at Cwmtydu (18), Ceibwr Bay (14), Abermawr (12) and Abereiddy (11). Seals are naturally inquisitive animals and you may find that one pops up close by when you're having a swim anywhere along the coast, especially in more sheltered coves. From around late August to November, several areas along the coast are home to seal pups and their mothers, including several of the places in this book. These adorable fluffy white creatures are quite helpless for the first few weeks of their lives and cannot survive in the sea, so their mothers find safe places for them to grow and gather strength. I have noted in each chapter the places where I know seal pupping may occur so that you can plan to avoid these places at that time of year. Please do respect this and behave responsibly around seals, paying attention to any local signage.

SEAL PUPPING SEASON

It is illegal to cause disturbances to seals. The general code of conduct is:

- Don't go onto beaches where pups are present.
- Do not approach, disturb or frighten seals.
- Keep all dogs on a lead if seals may be present.
- If you want to watch them, do it from afar, preferably where they cannot see you, and move on after 10 minutes of watching.
- Do not get between the adult seal and their pup. Females will often be close by, watching from the water.
- Do not chase them into the water.

After seals and dolphins, perhaps the next biggest draw to West Wales for wildlife enthusiasts is the birds. The West Wales coast, particularly around offshore islands, cliffs and stacks, has important breeding colonies of razorbills, guillemots, puffins, shearwaters, gulls, gannets, choughs and peregrine falcons, to name a few. My favourite places to spot sea birds are at Angle (Walk 4), St Non's (9) and Dinas Island (13).

If you're fond of birds you'll be happy to know that you may spot many different species during these walks: birds of prey such as red kites, buzzards, kestrels, peregrine falcons and ospreys; woodland birds like pied flycatchers, chiffchaffs, wood warblers, goldcrests and jays; and water birds such as geese, ducks, waders, dippers and kingfishers.

For a book about wild water, I've done a good job so far at not talking about fish. Sadly, fish populations are really struggling in Wales, as they are worldwide. Rivers once teeming in salmon and trout, and seas chock full of mackerel, herring and bass are now home to only meagre populations. One of the best ways to see what is around is to pack a snorkel or goggles and take a look underneath while you're swimming! The clear waters of the West Wales coast make for great snorkelling. One of the best places to watch salmon and trout migrating is at Henllan on walk 28.

Descending into Llangrannog

King's Quoit Burial Chamber, Manorbier

Other creatures you may be lucky enough to encounter are frogs, lizards, snakes, voles, otters, rabbits, hares, pine martins, deer and foxes. Some of these are more elusive but I've seen many on this list while out walking these routes.

The plant life in West Wales is rich and varied. From the mosses, lichens, liverworts and ferns of the Celtic Rainforest and the sphagnum moss, orchids, bog asphodel, cotton grass, bilberries and heather of the uplands; to the thrift, sea campion, squill, kidney vetch and bird's-foot trefoil of the coast path, there's always something new to discover. Why not pack a plant or bird ID book or download an identification app to connect with the nature on your walk and enrich your visits?

My advice for enjoying the wildlife in West Wales at its best is to go during quieter times, be curious, move quietly, make time to sit and absorb your surroundings, take some binoculars, tread gently and be respectful.

Heron at Bosherston

SAINTS AND STONES, POETS AND PRINCES

The history of West Wales is richer and more complex than I could ever summarise within the constraints of this book. Long at the frontier of what is now Wales, back when the sea was the main method of travel and trade, in the west we can discover traces going back to the Mesolithic period, when hunter-gatherers lived in seasonal settlements and were the first to begin altering the landscape on a large scale. Vast forests covered the land at that time, and traces of these can be seen at Borth on walk 19, Abermawr (12) and Manorbier (2).

Later, during the Neolithic and Bronze Ages, sophisticated civilization began to develop, and we can find remains of this in the many standing stones, burial chambers and stone circles that are present throughout the west; see two examples at Manorbier on walk 2 and St Davids Head (10).

The Iron Age saw an incredible number of hillforts built on promontories and hills throughout

Porthmelgan

Angle Peninsula

Below Carn Llidi

Dale

the region. Archaeological finds from various hill forts give proof of advanced societies and trading. There are too many hillfort remains to mention each one, but those you'll encounter at Solva on walk 8, Castell Bach (18), and at St Davids Head (10) are particularly noteworthy.

In the post-Roman era, the early Celtic Church flourished in West Wales. It is from this period, around the 6th and 7th centuries that some of our most celebrated saints appeared. Discover the stories of Wales' patron saint David and his mother St Non, in walk 9. St Carannog of Llangrannog appears in walk 17.

It is also during this time that some of the most fascinating of Welsh legends emerge. Learn more about the legends of royal bard Taliesin on walk 20, Gwyddno Garanhir the ruler of the lost land of Cantre'r Gwaelod, (19) and great leader and warrior Geraint of Dumnonia associated with Arthur (17).

Poetry has always been a defining feature of the history and culture of West Wales, and it's easy to understand why! The land here speaks poetry itself, and famed poets from early medieval bard Dafydd ap Gwilym, to Lewis Glyn Cothi, William Williams and, in later years, Dylan Thomas can all be found wandering through the pages of this book.

The Norman period, from 1066 to about 1300, was perhaps the most impactful in the way it shaped the West Wales we have today. Splitting the county of Pembrokeshire into south and north along a constantly changing but enduring border defended with castles known as the Landsker Line, southern Pembrokeshire became predominantly English speaking, while to the north the old language and customs were retained. Fierce battles were fought and land changed hands many times. One ruler in particular, Rhys ap Gruffudd, or Lord Rhys as he is widely known, prince of Deheubarth, a kingdom

St Non's

Musselwick Sands

which more or less included all of West Wales, put up a fearsome fight and retained control over the area for many years. Gerald of Wales, Gerallt Cymro in Cymraeg, descendant of both Welsh and Norman nobility, wrote extensively about the battles between the Anglo-Normans and the Welsh princes. Visit the castles, bishop's palaces, abbeys and cathedrals of this period at Manorbier on walk 2, Llawhaden (5), Tenby (1), St Davids (9), Strata Florida (24) and Cilgerran (15) to learn more.

A peace of sorts came to West Wales when Welsh king Henry Tudor ascended to the English throne. Born in Pembroke Castle, Henry had to flee to France to escape, before returning 14 years later, landing in Pembrokeshire at Mill Bay near Dale. From there, he was able to gather Welsh support and then to win the Battle of Bosworth to become king. Follow the story at Tenby on walk 1 and on the Dale Peninsula (6).

SHIPWRECKS AND SMUGGLERS, FOOD AND FLANNEL

In the Middle Ages, life in rural and coastal West Wales was hard, with farming, mining, fishing, ship building, weaving and metal working the main occupations. Goods such as lime and culm, a type of coal, were imported by boat to the harbours around the coast, and slate, stone, silver, copper and lead were quarried and extracted to be shipped out around the country. There is much evidence of these activities; almost every cove and harbour has the remains of a lime kiln. Mines such as those which you'll find in Cwm Rheidol on walk 22, at Abereiddy and Porthgain (11), Cwm Einion (20) and Dyffryn Castell (21), lay testament to these lost industries. Shipbuilding was an important trade and this maritime history is reflected in the fact that many coastal villages have pubs called 'Y llong', The Ship Inn. There was a darker side to this maritime trade, of course. The treacherous waters around the West Wales coastline have been the cause of many a tragedy over the years. Learn the stories of shipwrecks of the Albion on walk 7, Morning Star (14), Phoebe and Peggy (8), and HMS Barking (6).

Wild waters weren't the only dangers of the sea; renowned smugglers and pirates have long haunted the coastline of West Wales. Perhaps the most famous pirate of all, Barti Ddu, or Black Bart as he is more widely known, was a real-life pirate of the Caribbean, who was born between Fishguard and Haverfordwest. Causing trouble more locally was Captain Jack Furze in Manorbier, on walk 2, Boia in St Davids (9), Sion Cwilt in Cwmtydu (18). Walk through Smuggler's Valley Cwm Lladron on walk 17, and have a drink in East Angle at the old haunt of pirate John Callis (4).

One of the somewhat gentler occupations of the day was the production of wool, flannel and tapestries. Water was first used to drive wheels to power woollen mills, these often tucked away in the quiet wooded valleys of the West Wales coast,

Gwadn, Solva

Broadhaven South

particularly around Cardigan, Fishguard, St Davids and Drefach Felindre. Only a tiny fraction of the huge number of woollen mills remains, and you can visit these at Tregwynt on walk 12, and Drefach Felindre near Henllan (28).

The food of West Wales is some of the best in the country and almost every walk has an opportunity to try some delicious local cuisine. Fresh seafood and fish such as crab, lobster and mackerel is readily available along the coast. Pembrokeshire Early Potatoes, Laverbread and Velfrey sparkling wines all have protected status, and the milk, cheese, butter and ice cream produced across the region is renowned for its quality. Local orchards produce wonderful cider, and If I can get my hands on a cold bottle of Pembrokeshire Apple Juice after a long summer day walking on the coast path, I feel as though I've hit the jackpot.

WELSH WORDS

Cymraeg, the Welsh language, is spoken widely across West Wales, with the exception of southern Pembrokeshire where English has long been the dominant language. Welsh place names are beautifully poetic and often can tell us much about the place. Therefore it is well worth learning and using a few of them, and you'll see I've used Welsh place names throughout the book. I've listed some of the more topical words which you may come across in place names, on road signs and on the maps, below.

Pronunciation is not immediately straightforward, though once you know a few key rules it makes things a lot easier. At first glance, it appears that the Welsh language is not fond of vowels. In fact, Welsh has more vowels than English: 'y' and 'w' are both used as vowel sounds. Equally perplexing to non-Welsh speakers are the double letters. These are usually treated as a single letter in the Welsh alphabet. Here are a few general rules, to help you make sense of the pronunciation:

Ch – a soft, aspirated sound, as in the Scottish loch
Dd – similar to the th of 'these'
Ff – pronounce as an English 'f'
F – pronounce as an English 'v'
Ll – particularly difficult to master for non-Welsh speakers, put your tongue in the same position as you would to pronounce the 'l' sound in the word 'clean', but blow out slightly around the sides while saying it.
U – pronounce as 'ee'
W – when used as a vowel, it usually sounds similar to the English 'oo' in 'pool'.
Y – changes, depending on position. If near the beginning it is usually an English 'u', and 'i' if near the end of the word.

Using these rules, you can see that the pronunciation of the word for mountain, mynydd would be 'munith'; ddu, meaning black, is 'thee'; and sgwd, waterfall, is 'sgood'.

SOME WELSH WORDS FOR WALKERS AND SWIMMERS:

Aber – mouth of a river
Afon – river
Bach / fach – small
Cae – field or meadow
Caer – fortress
Castell – castle
Craig – rock or ridge
Cwm – valley
Dinas – settlement or fort
Du / Ddu – black
Dwr – water
Fawr / Mawr – large or broad
Llan – church or parish
Llech – stone, usually slate
Llyn – lake
Mynydd – mountain / hill
Nant – stream
Pen – peak or head
Perygl – danger
Pont – bridge
Porth – port or harbour
Pwll – pool
Sgwd or Rhaedr – waterfall
Traeth – beach

Wallog near Aberystwyth

ENJOYING THE WATER

People have been taking to the water for health, recreation and adventure for centuries in West Wales. From the Victorians who made their way to the coast in search of the health benefits of salt-water bathing, to the long-established swimming events such as the Solva Regattas, and the modern day Tenfoot, Long Course and Iron Man swims of Tenby and Saundersfoot. Coasteering, a pursuit exploring cliffs, caves, inlets and leaping off rocks into the sea, had its beginnings in Pembrokeshire at St Non's and Abereiddy. And in more recent years, the huge global cold water swimming community that is the Bluetits began life as a very small flock of winter sea swimmers in Porthselau near St Davids. Coast path walkers have long been cooling off their aching legs in the crystal waters of the remote coves along the west coast. To swim in West Wales is to follow in a long line of footsteps of those revelling in the beauty, simplicity and thrill of swimming in wild waters.

RIGHTS AND RESPONSIBILITIES

Whether through a usually-unfounded fear of liability, or through genuine concern for fragile water habitats, the welcome to swimmers in wild places can sometimes be as icy as the water. Although this is not the case on the coast, it is more so inland, where we have no protected legal right to access rivers, lakes or waterfalls. It is our responsibility, then, to be gentle in asserting our wishes to swim in wild waters, to show that swimmers do no more damage with our presence than the walkers, cyclists and anglers who have established rights to access and, indeed, that we can have a positive influence, advocating for the health of the aquatic habitats that we so treasure.

OUR WATERS UNDER THREAT

Though I have detailed the beauty, wildlife and all-round magic of each of the swimming spots

Teifi at Cilgerran

I have visited on the walks in this book, it would be remiss not to mention the negative influences that our wild waters are under. The Cleddau and Teifi rivers in particular, are under huge pressure from pollution caused by intensive agricultural practices, sewage releases, and drier springs and summers leading to low water levels. Our coastal waters are also at risk, with sewerage companies more regularly discharging untreated sewage into the sea. The benefits we feel from swimming wild, and the wildlife that calls these waters home are worth fighting for. As swimmers we can be advocates; there are numerous campaigns and citizen science projects that we can get involved with (see Further Information, below) And of course a good old-fashioned letter to your MP to voice your concerns about anything water-related can also be effective.

TREADING GENTLY

As lovers of wild spaces, we should all be endeavouring to follow the principles of Leave No Trace, and perhaps going further than that. Many swimming groups like to organise litter-picking events, and I usually carry a bag so that we can remove any litter we come across, providing it is safe to do so. If someone finds a spot litter-free, they are less likely to add to it. It also helps to smooth any tensions with landowners worried about swimmers causing damage, and keep our spots friendly and open. If you're looking to reduce your carbon footprint, and help reduce the volume of traffic in the countryside, consider whether you can travel on public transport. Many of the walks in this book have excellent public transport links, and have been designed to start near bus stops and train stations where possible.

In creating the walks in this book, I have followed Natural Resources Wales' Wild Swimming Code, as well as the Countryside Code. All of the walks are in areas where there is designated public access, including rights of way, access land and some waters with navigation rights. Here is a simplified version of their code; the full version can be found on their website (see Further Information).

DOWNLOADABLE ROUTE INFORMATION

For PDF and GPX route information to print out or transfer to your smartphone, use the last two words of each chapter introduction, with no spaces or capitals. For example, for Walk 1 go to **wildthingspublishing.com/westwales/thewalk**

WILD SWIMMING CODE

1. Respect others
Including walkers, anglers, landowners and other groups. If asked to leave by a landowner, move on without arguing. Change clothes discreetly if others are around. Keep noise to sociable levels.

2. Protect the environment
Avoid scuffing the river bed, tread lightly and avoid damaging vegetation. Minimise disturbance to birds particularly during the nesting season, livestock and other animals. Check, clean and dry your swimwear between different watercourses to avoid the spread of invasive species.

Llynnoed Ieuan

WALKING AND SWIMMING SAFETY

Pwll y Wrach, Moylgrove

Walking and wild swimming are not activities without their risks. Safety should be considered for your own sake and that of others. That said, these activities do not have to be dangerous, and by learning about the risks and how to protect yourself against them, you can minimise the chances of problems arising.

Where feasible, I have offered some hints and tips on safety at each location, so reading each walk's description is useful both before, and during your walk. However, it is impossible to list every single risk and hazard. The wild, dynamic environments in this book can change over time, so you will need to exercise your judgement and stay within your limits, which you know best. Please always err on the side of caution. Before setting off, consider three main safety aspects:

SKILLS AND KNOWLEDGE

The key to a successful and enjoyable walk is mostly in the planning. Researching routes, reading guide books (such as this one!) and looking at the map ahead of time will help you know what to expect, preferably with a nice cuppa in front of the fire. Self-selection of a route to suit your skills and knowledge is important, as only you know your capabilities. A good map is key, as well as map-reading skills. Some of the walks in this book are very easy to follow with paths and signposts, but others are more remote and need some navigation skills including being able to use a compass effectively. OS Explorer 1:25,000 scale maps are recommended. Bing Maps has a free-to-use OS map layer, and digital maps can be downloaded, including from the Wild Things website, though remember to do this before you set off, as many locations in the book do not have good signal coverage.

WEATHER AND CONDITIONS

Once you know where you're going, check the weather forecast, and keep checking it right up until the point that you're about to set off. For the coast, you can check the Met Office beach forecasts and tide times. The Met Office has a good surf report with details of swells and wind conditions. For the uplands I recommend using a specialist mountain forecast, due to the exaggerated conditions you'll find with even a moderate altitude gain. The Mountain Weather Information Service forecasts, and the Met Office Mountain Weather forecasts cover the Elenydd/Cambrian Mountains region. Be prepared, anyway, for the weather to turn unexpectedly, and carry the kit you need to keep yourself safe. Also consider what the weather has been like over the past few days as this will affect water conditions. You can check river levels on the River Levels UK website (details below).

On the coast path near Abereiddy

Mwnt

Swanlake Bay

KIT

Remote routes need a little more preparation: the further you go from roads, the more self-sufficient you'll need to be. Here is a non-exhaustive list of some of the clothing and equipment you should consider.

- Walking boots, sturdy, and preferably waterproof, with ankle protection.
- A waterproof coat and overtrousers will help to keep you dry and warm if the weather takes an unexpected turn.
- Food and water, more than you think you'll need.
- Spare layers of warm clothing.
- A personal first aid kit.
- A map and compass.
- A fully charged phone and back-up.
- Headtorch and emergency shelter for any unplanned delays in remote areas.
- Sealable dry bags can be used inside your rucksack help to stop everything from getting soaked in a downpour, though can be rather expensive; plastic bags rolled tightly down do just as good a job.
- Swimming requires very little equipment other than a towel, but a warm hat, some water shoes, a brightly coloured tow float and swim cap, and a flask of something warm to drink all help to make the experience more comfortable.

When you add swimming in cold water to your walk, you'll need to take some additional precautions and be self-sufficient in remote locations. Learning basic water safety will help you to avoid getting into difficulties.

WATER SAFETY TIPS

- Go with another competent swimmer or choose a lifeguarded beach
- Let someone know where you're going and when you expect to be back.
- Check for any obvious dangers in the area.
- Assess the volume and flow of the water, to ensure it is safe to enter.
- Avoid swimming after or during heavy rain, when water levels can rise suddenly, and debris and pollution may be present in the water. Never enter flood water.

- Avoid water that is clearly polluted. If you get in and realise afterwards that it is polluted, avoid getting any in your eyes, nose and mouth, get out and shower in clean water as quickly as possible. Before entering the water, check that you will be able to easily get out.
- Be prepared to change your plans if conditions aren't suitable.
- Wear shoes to protect your feet and move carefully on rocks near the water, which can be very slippery.
- Wear a tow float and brightly coloured swim cap if swimming in open water.
- Enter the water slowly initially, to acclimatise to the cold. Jumping straight in, even on a hot day can cause cold water shock, which can be fatal.
- Get out of the water before you begin to feel very cold, and get dressed quickly.
- Avoid hazards such as cliffs, the base of large waterfalls, weirs, structures or obstructions in the water.
- Before undertaking any jumps, check the water where you'll be jumping for depth and hidden objects. Don't assume it is safe to jump because you saw someone else doing it – they may have just been lucky.

If something does go wrong, if you're at the coast dial 999 and ask for the Coastguard. If you're in the mountains, dial 999 and ask for the police, then Mountain Rescue. Have ready as much information as you can about your location and details of the emergency.

Stackpole Quay

Porthmynawyd

Tidal pools, Porthclais

Llangrannog coastline

FURTHER INFORMATION

The following websites have a wealth of information for planning a safe, enjoyable and responsible swim walk. There are also links to a couple of social swimming groups, which can be great if you're new to wild swimming and looking for company.

LEAVE NO TRACE
lnt.org

NATURAL RESOURCES WALES WILD SWIMMING CODE
naturalresources.wales/days-out/the-countryside-codes/the-wild-swimming-code

ADVENTURESMART.UK
Safety campaign aiming to reduce the number of avoidable incidents which rescue & emergency services deal with in the outdoors.
adventuresmart.uk/wales

MOUNTAIN WEATHER INFORMATION SERVICE
mwis.org.uk

THE MET OFFICE
metoffice.gov.uk

RIVER LEVELS
A website where you can check water levels at various river stations.
riverlevels.uk

THE RIVERS TRUST
theriverstrust.org

SURFERS AGAINST SEWAGE
Grassroots ocean environment charity, produce a 'safer seas' water quality map
sas.org.uk

WILD SWIMMING
wildswimming.co.uk

OUTDOOR SWIMMING SOCIETY
outdoorswimmingsociety.com

THE BLUETITS
Local social swimming groups, with several across South Wales.
thebluetits.co

WILD TRAILS WALES
Guided walks, wild swims and navigation training in Wales
wildtrailswales.com

USEFUL APPS:
- Wales Coast Explorer
- Safer Seas and Rivers Service
- OS Maps
- iNaturalist
- Merlin or Birdnet

Pwllstrodur Bay

Walk 1

TENBY'S WILDER SIDE

Discover Tenby's wilder side on a walk that is breathtaking, both literally and figuratively, with a challenging section of coast path, peaceful wooded valleys and quiet sandy coves, to discover a world-class open water swimming destination.

Tenby is arguably Wales' most loved seaside holiday destination. Colourful houses perch on the clifftops, and visitors wander around a bustling walled town with souvenir shops, boat trips, and buckets-and-spades galore. Beyond the pretty facade is a rich and fascinating history: a medieval castle and defensive town walls, the Tudor Merchant's house, a secret medieval network of tunnels which helped a future king of England flee to safety, and a 19th century gun fort.

But if you're just here for the swimming and walking, you won't be disappointed. This pristine part of the Pembrokeshire coastline holds a boundless opportunity to enjoy the water, as well as fantastic walking on a challenging stretch of the coast path, and lesser-visited inland pathways. This route places Tenby in its centre, making it a perfect half-way stop for lunch or refreshments. If using public transport or staying in the town you can join the route from Tenby itself, and finish there.

Setting off through fields next to the popular campsite at Trevayne, the coast stretches out ahead. The steep pathway down to Monkstone beach suffered a small landslip recently and the way down was fenced off for a time, but even though a small fence is still in place, the path has now been repaired and you are able to pass around it. Do be aware that there is a final steep section to navigate with the help of a rope. As you climb down try not to think too much about the return journey, and definitely do not count the steps as that is a problem for later. First, delight in this beautiful curved stretch of golden sand, a tucked-away locals' favourite and one of the quietest in the area. Enormous cliffs of vertical rock

INFORMATION

This walk includes a challenging section of coast path, several sets of very steep steps, road crossings and muddy ground even in summer.

DISTANCE: 9½ miles
TIME: 4–5 hours not including swims or ice cream stops
MAP: OS Explorer OL36 South Pembrokeshire
START & END POINT: Park considerately at the pull-in near Trevayne campsite (SN 140 032, SA69 9DL). Alternatively join the route from the bus at New Hedges, or at Tenby itself.
PUBLIC TRANSPORT: Trains are available to Tenby. Bus 381 between Tenby and Haverfordwest stops at New Hedges near the start and end of the route.
SWIMMING: Monkstone Beach (SN 146 031), Waterwynch Bay (SN 137 020), Tenby North Beach (SN 133 009), Harbour Pier, seaward side – high tide only (SN 136 006), Castle Beach (SN 138 005), Tenby South Beach – lifeguarded in peak season (SS 131 999)
PLACES OF INTEREST: Tenby walled town, Tudor Merchant's House, Tenby castle, Tenby lifeboat stations, St Catherine's Island, lime kilns and tower at Kiln Park
REFRESHMENTS: Trevayne campsite (SA69 9DL, 01834 813402) has a great farm shop selling refreshments and goods produced on the farm and locally. Wide range of options in Tenby.

strata, densely vegetated, frame the beach, with views across the water to the Gower Peninsula and Tenby appearing to the west. Swimmers from the long distance Tenfoot Swim event come ashore here for a safety check and refreshment station en route from Tenby to Saundersfoot.

The centre of the beach is usually the best spot for a swim; just be aware of submerged rocks at high tide or that the bedrock may be more exposed after a recent storm. Low or mid tides are best here, though swimming is still possible at high tide; just take care not to become cut off from the exit if you are visiting during an incoming tide. If it is a hot day, you'll be glad of the shade of the trees on the way back up to the coast path, and thankful for the views back that you'll no doubt want to pause to take in from time to time.

Once you've regained the coast path ❷, enjoy a wonderful walk with far-reaching views through the wooded clifftops, over to Tenby and Caldey Island beyond. The path descends steeply and climbs again several times before arriving at a junction of paths. Turning down a narrow pathway you'll walk alongside a dreamy 19th century house, once the home of renowned painter Charles Norris. The land here was gifted to him in recognition of his work to promote Tenby as a tourism destination through his art. The beach is accessed via a narrow walkway alongside the house's tall stone walls. Strictly speaking all of the land above the Mean High Tide line is private, and this is marked approximately by the end of the slipway. It means that during high tide there is very little beach to play with, so a visit here is best enjoyed at low or mid tides. Swimming here is a delight; this small tucked-away sand and pebble cove is often sheltered and sunny during the middle of the day with large, smooth rocks to sunbathe on and a cave to explore at low tide.

A seemingly relentless climb follows ❸ and tops out next to an intriguing wooded area known as Allen's View, donated to Tenby Civic Society in the 1960s by Jessie Allen, who lived in neighbouring Clovers. This peaceful wooded spot has some impressive wooden carvings of birds which are fun to look at, and magnificent Monterey Pine trees, and is worth the very slight detour from the coast path, which it rejoins further down.

From here it is downhill all the way into the town. Dinbych y Pysgod, Tenby's Welsh name, means 'Little Fortress of the Fishes', the earliest known reference to this name dates back to the 9th century. A steep set of steps or, further on, a ramp, gives access to Tenby's wonderfully sheltered North Beach. The swimming potential is wonderful here, with a gently sloping sandy beach suiting everyone from dippers to long-distance swimmers. North Beach, in fact, is one of Wales' most well-known open water swimming destinations, with the Wales Swim event, part of the world-renowned Long Course Weekend (swimming, biking, running), being held here every June. Later, in September, the Ironman Wales triathlon comes to town, with the swim also held at North Beach. It is worth checking that these events don't coincide with your visit if you're hoping for a quiet swim!

Further along, at the harbour ❹, you'll pass St Julian's Church. This old fishermen's church was built to replace an earlier chapel where the services used to be led by the clergy from St Mary's, the main church in the centre of the town. They were reportedly paid in seafood to do so! In summer the church is sometimes open to visitors and it is worth a look inside to see the unique interior with fishing nets, lobsters and crabs adorning the walls.

Continue around the harbour ❺ where, at high tide in calm conditions, local youngsters gather

and jump into the water from the steps on the seaward side of the pier. Walking this route with my friend Nia who grew up in Tenby was fantastic as she was able to reminisce about the times she spent jumping off here with friends as a teenager. This is a great spot to enjoy the water, but water depth, hidden objects and sea conditions need to be carefully considered before jumping.

An optional loop of the castle hill gets you up close to the RNLI Lifeboat Stations. The newer building of the two is operational, opened in 2005. The castle remains themselves aren't hugely impressive, the original Norman castle losing importance after the town walls were built during the 13th century. Tenby flourished to become a major trading port, one of the best ways to learn more about this part of the town's history is by visiting the Tudor Merchant's house, tucked away in Quay Hill alleyway just above the harbour. The merchant town held a network of hidden tunnels leading from the walled town down to the Quay, and it is from the town that the future Henry VII fled Britain in 1471, to spend 14 years in exile ahead of returning and claiming the throne to found the Tudor dynasty.

For more swimming, head through the archway at the base of Castle Hill onto Castle Beach. At low tide this adjoins South Beach, a huge sweep of sand extending for a mile and a half. At high tide this is

a separate beach, with St Catherine's Island in the centre. The fort atop the island is Napoleonic, and was later used as a lavish residence and a zoo with squirrels, monkeys and reptiles. Today the fort lies empty, but visitors can climb the steps onto the island and explore inside for a small fee.

Otherwise, take the main route into the town, and through the cobbled streets, where there are plenty of chances to stop for a bite to eat or a drink. Then leave the walled town behind and walk along the clifftop promenade, lined with colourful houses and seafront hotels. A ramp at the end of the promenade leads down to South Beach, which, more exposed than the others, makes for great fun playing in the waves. This beach is lifeguarded during peak times, so it is a great option if you are a less confident swimmer. Don't be afraid to chat to the lifeguards for information about the beach and advice, and swim between their flags. If you prefer things a little quieter, wander down the beach a little and you'll soon discover its wilder side.

If you're joining from the bus, train, or from your base in Tenby, this is where you'll begin and end the walk ❻. The route goes past the golf course and over the rail line into the expansive Kiln Park caravan and holiday park. Named after the enormous lime kilns here, which you'll walk past, and are really very impressive, this area was once home to a large-scale limestone quarry and lime production site.

After the hustle and bustle of the town, its popular beaches and the holiday park, the route now enters an altogether different environment, one of wetlands, meadows and trees ❼. Even on a sunny summer weekend you'll encounter very few other people on this beautiful inland path through the Knightston Brook wooded valley ❽. Luxuriate in the birdsong and lush green canopy, a peaceful contrast to the town. Reaching New Hedges ❾, a final climb through the village and a wander along a flower-lined lane takes you back to Trevayne and the end of the walk.

DIRECTIONS

❶ Take the permissive path through the gateway of Trevayne campsite, then turn left to go through the barns. Go through the gate into the field slightly to the right and aim for the trees ahead, walking next to the hedge on the left. At the junction of paths, take the right-middle path. At time of writing there is still a wooden fence here, from when the works were being done on the path previously, but you are able to bypass it. The path soon begins descending steeply on steps, follow it down through trees to the beach for a first swim.

0.4 miles

❷ Return to the top of the path and turn left, taking the coast path south then south-west. When you descend into the second wooded valley, cross the footbridge then take a left-hand turn, taking the footpath signposted to the beach. Walk down the narrow passageway to reach Waterwynch Bay for a second swim.

1.7 miles

❸ Follow the footpath back to the path junction then turn left, following the coast path sign, climbing uphill on a semi-paved path. At the top of the path take a left into Allen's View, and walk through the woods, rejoining the coast path at the far end. Turn left and follow the path and steps downhill, coming out onto a lane and passing a hotel on your left. Continue on this lane until you reach the steps down to North Beach on your left or continue further to take the ramp down to the beach instead, the third swim location.

0.9 miles

❹ Climb back up and take the path at the southern end of North Beach to the harbour. Follow the harbour round to the pier on the seaward side to find a small set of steps for another swim.

0.7 miles

❺ Go through the archway next to the harbour to Castle Beach, for the seventh swim spot. Return back to the arch, turn left and follow St Julian's Street towards the town centre, turning left before the bookshop on Cob Lane to The Paragon. Continue along the clifftop lane and behind the hotel then go through the archway, turning left towards the sea front. Follow the Esplanade to the end, then take a left down the path leading on to the beach, for the sixth and final swim spot.

0.7 miles

❻ Return back to the path at the play park, and turn left, following a sign for the train station. Follow the cycle route and coast path signs south-west past the golf course, then take a right over a railway bridge into the caravan park. Bear right then left past the shop. Keep left here then take the

right fork as you go past the tennis court and tower. Continue past the kilns to the exit.
1.3 miles

❼ Cross the road next to the garage and look for a footpath into the wetlands opposite. Turn right and follow the path through wetlands, meadows and woodland. At a footbridge with a path junction, take the left. Shortly you'll reach the B-road. Turn right and follow this road for a short section, being aware of fast-moving vehicles as there is no pavement here.
0.6 miles

❽ Cross the road onto a farm track. At a fork in the track turn left and go through the gate on the left onto a footpath through woodland. Continue on this path through the woodland, with the brook always away to the left. Reach a railway bridge and walk beneath it, turning left. After a short distance, turn right so you are now walking east. Follow the path through the woods until it emerges onto a farm track. Turn right along the lane and continue past the campsite onto the main road.
1.9 miles

❾ Cross the main road then take a path straight ahead into the village. Turn left on the main road through the village and follow the road uphill. Turn right onto the lane marked 'Trevayne and Campsite' just before you get to the main road junction. Follow the road to the end to return to the start.
1 mile

Walk 2

SKRINKLE AND MANORBIER

A superlative walk packed with history and colourful characters, not to mention sandy hidden bays, traditional countryside, a medieval castle and stunning clifftop panoramas.

As you approach the beginning of the route, you'd be forgiven for thinking it an unlikely setting for a beautiful swim-walk – but stick with it and you'll soon be glad you did. Before setting off, climb up slightly from the car park to the cliff top and, with the breathtaking vantage over Skrinkle Bay, all becomes clear. From here the dense vegetation on the cliffs, together with the golden sand and turquoise waters, lends a tropical air to the place.

There's a fair descent to reach the beach, including a steep set of stone steps and a metal grid staircase at the very bottom. It's best to time your visit here at low tide, and be aware that the sands shift here at different times of year; after autumn and winter storms there may not be very much sand at all on the beach and you'll have to negotiate slippery seaweed-covered rocks, especially higher up the beach. There's a magnificent archway, known as the 'Church Doors' in the cliff with vertical strata of limestone sandwiched seemingly impossibly at the top of the archway. At low tide in summer there is a perfect patch of golden sand in the cove. The beach slopes steeply so the water quickly becomes deep. At low tide strong swimmers could swim round to the deserted Swanlake Bay, or for a real adventure there is a cave running through the point between the two beaches that it's possible to scramble through. This is not without danger though. You may want to pay heed to the signs that are everywhere warning against doing this due to the difference in height of the two beaches; the water will be much higher on the other side and there is no escape from the other side other than the way you came.

After a swim here, warm up by climbing back up the steep steps to join the coast path ❷, and follow it to the gates of the still

INFORMATION

Some steep climbs up and down to beaches on steps and slopes. Rough terrain on the coast path which gets close to the cliff edge in places. Beaches can be prone to strong currents and submerged rocks. Toilets halfway, at Manorbier.

DISTANCE: 7 miles
TIME: 3 hours not including swims or stops
MAP: OS Explorer OL36 South Pembrokeshire
START & END POINT: Skrinkle Haven Car Park (SS 083 976, SA70 7TT)
PUBLIC TRANSPORT: Trains between Swansea and Pembroke stop at Manorbier, a couple of miles north of the beach. Otherwise, the nearest train station is Tenby. The 349 bus runs between Tenby, Haverfordwest and Pembroke, and stops at Skrinkle Estate less than a mile from the beginning of the route.
SWIMMING: Skrinkle Bay / Church Doors Cove (SS 081 974), Swanlake Bay (SS 045 980), Manorbier Bay (SS 060 975), Presipe Beach (SS 069 970)
PLACES OF INTEREST: Church Doors cliff formation, Manorbier Castle, King's Quoit burial chamber
REFRESHMENTS: The YHA's Skrinkle café (SA70 7TT, 01834 871803) offers drinks and snacks to visitors at selected times. The Castle Inn at Manorbier (SA70 7TE, 01834 871268) serves pub food and often has live music. The tea room in the castle (SA70 7SY, 01834 870 081) is good for drinks and cakes. For something special book ahead for the Rhosyn restaurant at Penally Abbey (SA70 7PY, 01834 843033).

active military base, originally a much larger camp, established post-World War II as an anti-aircraft artillery training school. Some of the former camp buildings have been repurposed into the YHA hostel set just above Skrinkle Bay.

Instead of following the right of way on the map, which has access issues – there's often barbed wire, with gates padlocked ¬– continue further along the lane to the housing estate and walk through the recreational field ❸ to reach a pretty green lane which takes you into the village of Manorbier.

Manorbier is the definition of whimsical: a village of pretty stone cottages, a whitewashed medieval church, an impossibly romantic beach and dunes, all overlooked by a magnificent castle. The route takes you right past the entrance of the castle and it's possible to go inside if you pay a small entry fee, well worth it if you have the time.

The castle was established here in the late 11th century by the Norman Knight Odo de Barri, under the Lordship and Earldom of Pembroke. This was a stronghold for the Normans in Wales since the invasion in 1066. The castle was strengthened by subsequent generations of de Barris and much of what can be seen today dates back to the 13th century. The most famous of the castle's residents was Gerald of Wales, a descendant of both Norman and Welsh nobility. Born in the castle in 1146, he became a priest and historian, not to mention Clerk to the King and advisor on Welsh affairs. His written works provide some of the most important insights of life in 12th century Wales and Ireland. Not just a prolific scholar, Gerald was dedicated to the church and in particular to campaigning for a Welsh church to be independent of Canterbury, reporting directly to Rome. He spent much of his life in pursuit of the position of Bishop of St David's. He was scuppered at each attempt for political reasons and because of his stance in support of the Welsh. There is far more to his story than can be covered here and it is well worth reading up on the exploits of this most fascinating figure in Welsh history.

Gerald of Wales is not the only character associated with Manorbier. In the early 19th century, a sailor, Captain Jack Furze, arrived into Manorbier, claiming to have saved money and wanting to lease the land around the castle to farm and mine as a change of lifestyle. He was welcomed by the locals and settled down, though he still kept a boat, The Jane, a sailing brig which he would take out along the coast regularly. The farming and mining, of course, was a front for his smuggling operation, using the castle's cellars and passageways for storing contraband. One day one of the King's ships caught up with The Jane as Furze was sailing her along the coast, and began firing. Legend has it that Furze sent his entire crew below deck to shelter, and he steered the ship alone, all the while dodging shots. Darkness began to fall and the King's ship pulled back in fear of the dangers of navigating the coastline at night. Captain 'Jolly' Jack got away with it, though this close call was enough to make him change his ways and give up the smuggling life for good.

Leaving Manorbier behind, for now, a quiet lane ❹ leads away from the beach. A footpath at the top of the hill takes you into farmland then back to the coastline above Swanlake Bay. Often very quiet and peaceful, being accessible only on foot, Swanlake is a beautiful sweep of red-gold shingle and sand backed by Red Sandstone cliffs and lush farmland. There are rockpools and inlets to explore, and it's possible to swim here at all stages of the tide; at low tide the western end of the beach is the most sheltered.

From the beach there is a climb back uphill to gain the clifftop on the coastal path ❺, and an enjoyable walk along the coast with a bird's eye

view over the sea back to Manorbier, where you'll emerge next to the beach. The beach at Manorbier is popular with surfers thanks to the waves which roll in here and the relative ease of access. A fixed rip current runs under the rocks on the left-hand side of the beach as you look out to sea, so avoid swimming there. On the right-hand side of the beach waves crash onto the rocks, making it unsafe for swimming unless in very calm conditions. So, the middle of the beach is usually the best option, and it is an enchanting setting for a splash in the waves, in the shadow of the castle.

The beach holds traces of a much more distant period of history, one in which what is now the coastline would have been inland, looking out over a forested plain. At very low tides and after storms remains of peat beds and drowned forests have been spotted here, from a time when sea levels were lower.

Once you've had your fill of the beach, rejoin the coast path ❻ which snakes around the beach on the cliffside, passing the King's Quoit, a 5,000-year-old Neolithic burial chamber in a spectacular location overlooking the sea. A huge capstone sits at an angle supported by two upright stones.

The coast path from here is truly spectacular. A head for heights is an asset here, or just don't look down! Before reaching the military base there is a set of steps leading very steeply down to the final swim spot on the walk, Presipe Beach. A sandy bay revealed at low tide lies below Red Sandstone cliffs, in the same vertical beds as at neighbouring Skrinkle. Trace fossils can be found in the exposed rock layers. In calm conditions this is Paradise Found; the water is crystal and the sand is soft underfoot. When there is swell and at high tide, the water can bounce around between the rocks and make conditions trickier, so use your judgement here.

After climbing back up from the beach ❼ there's just a short walk around the back of the military base to return to the start.

DIRECTIONS

❶ From the furthest end of the car park walk up to the clifftop to see the view over Skrinkle Haven below. Then take the coast path with the sea on your left, downhill through trees until you reach a set of steps on your left leading down to the beach. Follow those, steeply downhill, to reach the cove.

0.2 miles

❷ Return to the top of the steps then follow the Wales Coast Path left, at first skirting just above the beach then turning inland through fields to meet the lane. Turn left on the lane towards the gate of the military camp, then turn right and follow the lane towards the housing estate on your right. Ignore the footpath sign on your left, instead continue further then turn into a recreational field on your left. Walk straight across the field heading to the south-west corner where there is a gate onto a track through some woodland.

0.9 miles

❸ Follow the track through the woodland then continue when it emerges onto a lane between houses. When you reach a crossroads at the end of the lane, turn left and follow the lane downhill, with the castle up on your right, all the way to the beach car park.

0.6 miles

❹ Continue on the lane past the car park, as it heads above the beach. Don't turn off onto the coast path but instead continue to the top of the hill where a footpath leads into fields on the left. Follow this past East Moor farm, then shortly after turn left towards the sea, and zig-zag down the hill to reach Swanlake Bay. There is a small and easily managed scramble down onto the beach.

1.3 miles

❺ Return to the Wales Coast Path and turn right, heading eastwards uphill, then following the path first south, then westwards again. Follow the path as it hugs the coast; you'll emerge on to the beach at Manorbier.

1.5 miles

❻ Walk to the far side of the beach and up the rocks to gain the coast path, which snakes closely alongside the coastline above the beach, past the King's Quoit burial chamber. Continue on the coast path for some time until you see a set of steps heading downhill to Presipe Beach. Go down the steps to get to the beach at low tide.

1.2 miles

❼ Return to the coast path and follow it diagonally uphill across the fields until you reach the edge of the military camp. The path takes you around the perimeter of the camp, and you'll come out on the lane next to the camp entrance. Continue on the lane ahead towards the YHA, either taking the lane to return to the car park or rejoining the coast path on the right, retracing your earlier steps to arrive back at the car park that way.

1.3 miles

Walk 3

STACKPOLE

This is a walk of contrasts, from the serene Bosherston Lily Ponds, to dramatic clifftops. Visit two of Pembrokeshire's most loved sandy beaches, hidden coves revealed at low tide and caves, as well as a tiny quay, flower-topped cliffs and woodland.

INFORMATION

Coast path with some steep slopes and steps; expect mud, sandy paths, rocks, tracks and grassy clifftops. Some minor rock scrambling to reach one of the coves. Toilets halfway at Stackpole Quay.

DISTANCE: 6½ miles
TIME: 3 hours not including swims
MAP: OS Explorer OL36 South Pembrokeshire
START & END POINT: Broadhaven Beach car park (SR 976 939, SA71 5DZ)
PUBLIC TRANSPORT: Bus 387 / 388 from Pembroke Dock, connecting with trains, calls at Broadhaven South on Tuesdays, Thursdays and Saturdays. Or use the Fflecsi service (https://tfw.wales/fflecsi).
SWIMMING: Small bay south of Broadhaven (SR 977 936), Broadhaven Bay (SR 979 939), Stackpole Quay (SR 993 957) and Barafundle Bay (SR 991 950)
PLACES OF INTEREST: Devil's Quoit standing stone, lily ponds, Five Arch Bridge
REFRESHMENTS: On the route is the wonderful Boathouse National Trust tea rooms (SA71 5LS, 01646 623110) with all the delicious cakes, cream teas, sandwiches and soups that you'd expect. A mile or so off route but well worth a visit is the Stackpole Inn (SA71 5DF, 01646 672324), an award-winning pub and restaurant with an emphasis on local produce and fresh fish. St Govan's Inn in Bosherston (SA71 5DN, 01646 661792) is a more laid-back pub option, good, catering for different dietary requirements.

Best known for jewel-in-the-crown Barafundle Bay, this small area of the South Pembrokeshire coast has so much to explore that you could spend several days here and still not see it all. This walk takes in the much-loved sandy bays at Broadhaven and Barafundle, but you'll also explore sand dunes, cliff tops, hidden low-tide coves, caves, lily ponds, woodland and farmland. The walk is just six miles long, but with so much to see and explore, start early and spend a full day here, walking and swimming to your heart's content.

Our route begins at Broadhaven South, where there is a moderate-sized National Trust car park (with toilets), and where the buses stop ❶. Instead of walking down to Broadhaven South beach straight away, for our first swim of the day we head west to a little cove below the farm campsite. A small path leads down onto the rocks where you can swim and snorkel around the cove in the crystal blue waters.

After returning to the coast path ❷, it's time to explore Broadhaven South beach, a piece of beach paradise, with a swathe of soft golden sand backed by dunes, hugged by steep limestone cliffs, and with the stone stack known as Church Rock watching over the bay from out at sea. The bay is a wonderful place to swim with clear water and a more sheltered spot next to Star Rock on the southern end of the bay. At mid-tide this is a great spot for jumping off into the water. To the eastern end of the bay at low tide, strong, confident swimmers can explore Saddle Point, where there is an

enormous blue hole, formed when the roof of a cave made by the sea collapsed. Turquoise water fills the bottom of the hole. Swim into it through a narrow arch, only accessible at low-tide, and in calm conditions, being wary of the strong currents around the point. The arch is submerged at high tide, so great care should be taken not to become stranded inside the hole from where there is no escape and where you could find yourself treading water until the tide recedes again!

Contrasting greatly with all the drama of Broadhaven and its cliffs and windblown sand dunes, is the serenity of Bosherston Lily Ponds ❸. The ponds were created by the Campbell family, Lords of Cawdor and owners of the Stackpole Estate in the 18th century, by damming up one of the streams which flowed through the valley. This was part of a huge landscaping project to completely remodel the estate. The result is a large lake with several arms extending inland, filled with the blooms of hundreds of water lilies during summer, with dragonflies humming by, swans gliding gracefully past with a trail of fluffy grey cygnets in their wake, and herons standing guard on the banks of the pond. It might be a wonderful place to swim, if it wasn't for the fact that it is also so well known for its pike fishing. Good to know perhaps, before you risk a cheeky dip here! The ponds are also known as one of the best places to spot otters in Wales; come early in the morning or late in the evening and move quietly for the best opportunity to see them. I once saw a large otter at the outflow of the ponds next to the beach on an early morning walk whilst staying at Trefalen Farm campsite.

Our route takes us up to the 18th century eight-arched stone bridge ❹, near the site of the Cawdor's court house. The enormous Georgian Palladian court was built in the 1730s, on the site of an earlier fortified manor dating back to the late medieval period. This work was so extensive that the entire village of Stackpole had to be relocated to its current position to make way for the court. It was of such grandeur that it was considered the most prestigious residence in Wales and compared to that of royalty. Sadly, the house fell into disrepair after the Second World War, and was demolished in 1963. In the 1970s the ponds and coastline were passed into the ownership of the National Trust.

If you continue without crossing the bridge, you'll reach a hide which is a lovely spot to sit for a while and birdwatch. Crossing the bridge, our route takes us through some verdurous dairy pasture, where you'll likely see large herds of cows grazing. There are electric fences separating cows from the path, which is a National Trust permissive path. A path to the right heads towards the woods which are full of ramsons and bluebells in spring. Just beyond the woods in a field is a mysterious 1.7-metre-high standing stone known as the Devil's Quoit. It has been dated back to the Bronze Age and is one of

several prehistoric structures discovered in the area spanning more than a thousand years.

We retrace our steps back to the main track ❺, which takes us to the National Trust car park at Stackpole Quay. There is a tea room here which serves excellent food and drinks and is a well-timed pitstop, halfway round the route. Just below the tea room is the quay, which is a popular launching point for kayaks. If you can time your visit here to high tide, you'll be able to swim in the sheltered waters of the quay, keeping an eye out for other water users. Lots of people including coasteering groups jump off the quay at high tide but, as with any big jump, you really do need to make sure the water is deep enough before doing this.

Stackpole Quay is not only popular with water sports enthusiasts and swimmers, but it is also an area of particular interest to geologists: here it is possible to see very clearly the boundary between the Old Red Sandstone from the Devonian and Silurian geological periods, and the Carboniferous Limestone. In lay terms, the reddish-purple rocks to the north and the grey rocks to the south come from different geological eras. It is fascinating to contemplate the layers of time and environments involved in the formation of these rocks. There is also a geological fault visible in the quay.

Leaving the quay behind ❻, we climb on to the clifftops, towards a large stone wall, demarking the deer park once established here as part of the estate. For so many people, it's the view down on to Barafundle Bay which captures their hearts, and makes it number one on so many 'top beaches' lists. It really is beautiful and the sheltered sea backed by dunes and surrounded by trees is a sight to behold.

The sea here is great for a dip or a lengthier swim up and down the bay, but there is plenty of exploring to be done too. At low tide find caves in

the cliffs to the north-east of the beach, and paddle around to a hidden bay. Another cave, marked as Lorts Cave on the map, is named after Roger Lort, who was the owner of the Stackpole Estate during the 1600s. Stackpole was besieged, and legend has it that Royalist Roger hid in this cave to evade capture. After the Restoration, Lort was made a Knight in return for his loyalty to the throne. Another adventure for strong swimmers is to swim out to the cliff arches named Griffith Lorts Hole, another feature named after the Lort family.

We finish up our walk by climbing up through the trees ❼ and out on to the Stackpole Warren headland, a National Nature Reserve. Rabbits were once farmed here extensively. Whether for food or sport it isn't known, but their descendants can still be seen lolloping in the bracken and heather. Look out for choughs, peregrine falcons and guillemots, razorbills and fulmar, all of which nest on the vertiginous cliffs below the headland. Just before you return to Broadhaven beach ❽ don't miss the fantastic birds' eye view of the blue hole from the clifftops above.

DIRECTIONS

❶ Walk south through the car park, crossing through a small gap at the end. Turn slightly right to walk diagonally through a grassy area to reach the coast edge. Take the path down onto the rocks of the cove below for a first swim.
0.1 miles

❷ Return to the coast path and turn right, following it with the sea on your right to the toilet / information building above Broadhaven South beach. Take the path on the right leading down to the beach.
0.3 miles

❸ Walk to the far end of the beach and walk inland, north-west, following the small stream to a footbridge. Cross the footbridge then turn left, on a good path with the lily ponds on your left. Cross the bridge at the end of the path and turn right, following a path through woodland next to the lily pond which is now on your right. Continue until the eight-arched bridge.
1.2 miles

❹ Cross the bridge and follow a track through the centre of some fields, looking for a path on your right leading into the woods. Go down the path into the woods then continue straight ahead, out of the woods and into a field. Turn right to visit the standing stone.
0.7 miles

❺ Retrace your steps back through the woods and out into the fields, rejoin the track and turn right.

Follow the track all the way to the car park. Go through the car park, past the toilets and tea rooms, and continue past the steps on the right through the trees to a rocky ledge, where a metal ladder descends onto the small beach next to the quay. Alternatively head straight down to the cove below the tea rooms.
1 mile

❻ From the rocks / ladder, retrace your steps then turn left to go up the steps heading south. Follow the path close to the fence line on your right, then go through the gap in the stone wall ahead and down the steps to reach Barafundle Bay.
0.5 miles

❼ At the far south end of the beach, a faint path leads up into the trees, up some steps then out onto the warren. There is a shortcut directly across the headland, but for the best views hug the cliff edge, keeping the sea to your left, until you reach a wall and gate above Broadhaven. If you're steady on your feet and it is low tide you can scramble down the rocks and paddle through the stream to take a shortcut back on to the beach. Otherwise continue ahead through the dunes following the wall, to return to the footbridge at the end of the lily ponds.
2.2 miles

❽ Walk across the beach and back up the path and steps to return to the car park.
0.4 miles

Walk 4

ANGLE PENINSULA

Visit Freshwater West, a famous film location and surfing beach, walk along wild clifftops, discover abandoned forts, swim in a pretty sand cove, and delight in the area's unique flavours on this long, circular treasure-trove of a walk.

The Angle Peninsula stands sentry over the Milford Haven waterway, one of the deepest natural harbours in the world. Our walk around this peninsula delves into a surprising variety of environments, from the swell-sculpted sandy beach at Freshwater, to the tranquil horseshoe bay of West Angle, jagged clifftops and the serene sheltered estuary at East Angle.

We begin at the Broomhill Burrows car park, but you can join this walk at various points along the route using the bus, depending on what works best for you.

Broomhill Burrows is one of the largest sand dune systems in Pembrokeshire and a designated Site of Special Scientific Interest. As you wander the path through the dunes to the sea, you may be lucky enough to spot some rare plants such as sea spurge, dune fescue, golden samphire or rock sea-lavender in the stony strandline as you reach the beach. The dunes support rabbits, adders, lizards and two rare species of moth.

As you emerge on to the beach, it may begin to look familiar. Harry Potter fans will instantly recognise this as the location of the shell house in the film of Harry Potter and the Deathly Hallows. The shell house which was constructed for filming was dismantled afterwards, but people come from far and wide to pay homage at 'Dobby's grave', a location in the dunes where the elf character was buried. Unfortunately, some visitors have left a terrible mess and the National Trust is working hard to manage the site in line with its Leave No Trace principles.

Freshwater West was also the location for the iconic 2010 Robin Hood film starring Russell Crowe, in a scene which saw

INFORMATION

Rugged coast path terrain with several steep climbs, slopes, mud, sand dunes and one section of road. Toilets at West Angle Bay and Freshwater West.

DISTANCE: 10 miles
TIME: 5 hours not including swims or stops
MAP: OS Explorer OL36 South Pembrokeshire
START & END POINT: Broomhill Burrows car park, Freshwater West (SM 884 005, nearest post code SA71 5HW). Larger car park and toilets further to the south at Gupton Burrows.
PUBLIC TRANSPORT: The 387 Coastal Cruiser bus stops at Freshwater West, West Angle Bay and East Angle on its circular route from Pembroke. Less frequent service out of the main summer season.
SWIMMING: Sandy beaches Freshwater West (SM 880 003), and West Angle Bay (SM 853 032). Rocky cove for calm conditions only at West Pickard Bay (SM 862 012), and tidal lagoon near West Angle Bay (SM 852 034) with high tide coasteering.
PLACES OF INTEREST: Dobby's Grave, seaweed drying hut (just off route), East blockhouse, Thorn Island Fort, Chapel Fort, The Old Point House pirates' inn
REFRESHMENTS: The Wavecrest café at West Angle Bay is a popular little spot and is great for cakes, coffees, sandwiches and ice creams (SA71 5AZ, 01646 641457). The Old Point House, in East Angle is a cosy 16th century inn right on the water's edge (SA71 5AS, 01646 792100).

more than a hundred horses galloping along the beach in a battle scene.

Meanwhile, Freshwater West is perhaps best known as the home of the best surfing waves in Wales; it has hosted the annual Welsh National Surfing Championships since the 1960s. The swell can indeed be enormous here, and there can also be strong and dangerous rip currents. The beach is lifeguarded during the busy summer season at its southern end where there are also toilet facilities and often a catering van, so head there for advice from the lifeguards. Confident, strong swimmers who are good at reading water conditions will enjoy playing in the waves; this is a huge beach and there is an unparalleled sense of space, freedom and awe to be found amongst the salt, sand and sunshine here.

If you do venture down to the southern end of the beach, above the rocks ahead of you, is a rectangular thatched hut on the grassy clifftops. This is the last remaining hut of some 20 once found here, used for drying seaweed in the early 20th century. During this time there was a cottage industry of women from Angle who harvested laver, an edible seaweed, from the rocks here. The seaweed was dried on the floor of the huts, then sent to Swansea, where it was used for making laverbread. The local industry ceased around the 1940s, but in recent years there has been a revival of the use of seaweed for culinary purposes. This has been driven greatly by the efforts of the Pembrokeshire Beach Food Company, which also had a hugely successful pop-up catering unit in the main car park for several years. The Café Môr has now relocated alongside the owner's new venture at the Old Point House in East Angle and is well worth a visit to sample seafood and seaweed-infused dishes; our route passes right by later on.

Back at the northern end of the beach, we re-enter the dunes and join the coast path going north. There is an ominous sign here warning walkers of rugged, remote, committing terrain ahead. In truth, the going isn't particularly tougher than other sections of the Pembrokeshire Coast Path, but it is rollercoaster-like, with ups and downs to test your legs, and several miles without an escape route onto a road. The only way off the path is back the way you came, or to carry on. Pack plenty of water and some snacks to keep you going.

The coastline here is breathtakingly beautiful, with crooked fingers of rock pointing into the frothing sea. Numerous sea arches, and islands with unimaginative yet descriptive names like Thorne Island, Rat Island and Sheep Island have been cut off from the shoreline through the incessant weathering actions of the sea over thousands of years.

Between East Pickard Bay and West Pickard Bay, the path passes alongside an Iron Age fort, with an obvious ditch and rampart visible - West Pickard Camp.

It isn't until you reach a gully after West Pickard Bay that you reach another potential swim spot in the rocky cove. Drop down on the rocks through the centre of the gully to reach the water, assessing conditions carefully to make sure you're comfortable getting in, being in and getting out of the water again; help is a long way off! On a calm day this can be a phenomenal spot for snorkelling. The Old Red Sandstone almost glows against the cobalt of the sea here on a sparkling summer day.

❷ The clifftop views keep on giving, a wild frontier against the open ocean, then, gently, as you round the tip of the peninsula near Rat Island, civilisation feels very present. Here there are the remains of an old blockhouse, balanced precariously on a narrow section of cliff. This was constructed during the 1860s on the orders of Lord Palmerston, Prime Minister at the time,

and looked over to a twin blockhouse to the west at Dale. They were both there to guard the ports of Milford Haven and Pembroke.

Soon we arrive at West Angle Bay, a gorgeous sandy beach popular with swimmers and for all kinds of water sports. Swimming here is a delight, and possible at all levels of the tide. West Angle Bay is another Site of Special Scientific Interest, home to the cushion starfish, a small plump green species only identified in the 1970s. The bay is also one of the most important sites for the understanding of glacial chronology in Wales. The geology doesn't fit the expected sequence and there is no consensus on how the rocks ended up the way they are here!

There is a fantastic, secret sheltered lagoon just off the bay which fills up at high tide and has a channel between the rocks which is great fun for jumping into; just check the depth as it varies with the tide. This is a wild swimming paradise and one of the highlights of the walk so try to time your visit for high tide to enjoy it at its best.

Leaving West Angle Bay on the coast path ❸, we reach a point off which lies Thorne Island. This is home to an impressive fort built during the Napoleonic years as one of Milford Haven's defences. In subsequent years the fort was converted to a hotel, and over the last couple of decades a succession of development attempts faltered. It is currently in private ownership.

One of at least 12 wrecks in the vicinity, in 1894 the sailing ship Loch Shiel ran ashore off Thorne Island. En route from Scotland to Adelaide, the ship contained cargo including vast quantities of whisky. The passengers and crew were saved by the Angle Lifeboat, whose crew received medals of honour. Much of the cargo went down with the ship, and two men died attempting to retrieve some of it, as well as one who died of alcohol poisoning. In recent years divers have retrieved bottles of beer from the wreck which sold at auction for £1,000!

We continue along the coast path, with the striking cylindrical Stack Rock fort in view out to sea, and pass Chapel Fort on land ❹, which hosts a military museum. Rounding the easterly point of the peninsula, the estuary waters stretch out ahead, and the sheltered West Angle Bay then comes into view ❺. Muddy and not really suitable for swimming, this is nevertheless a lovely spot: a paradise for wading birds and a real sun trap. Not without its own drama though, this was said to be one of the favourite haunts of notorious pirate John Callis, who apparently hid out at the Point House pub in an attempt to evade the law. Follow in his footsteps and stop for a pint and some seafood in the fantastic beer garden ❻, before continuing up the flower-lined lanes and fields ❼, to Freshwater West.

DIRECTIONS

❶ Walk through the sand dunes to reach the beach, with an option to walk southwards to the lifeguarded area during summer, and to visit Dobby's grave and the seaweed drying hut. Return to the north end of the beach and join the coast path heading west, keeping the sea on your left. Continue past East Pickard and West Pickard Bays to a narrow valley with stream running through. Drop down on to the rocks to explore the cove.
1.8 miles

❷ Return to the coast path and continue, hugging the cliffs heading west, north then east, all the way to West Angle Bay. The path brings you out next to the café; access the beach in front of the café.
3.1 miles

❸ Continue on the coast path which turns west again, on the north side of the bay. There's a path down to the small lagoon on your left. The path turns eastwards, and continues to follow the coast with the sea on your left, then turns right, then left, to go behind Chapel Bay fort.
1.1 miles

❹ Continue with woodland on your left, all the way to the lifeboat station, and beyond, into some fields before you round the East Angle Point, and come out onto a track, which passes the Old Point House inn.
1.2 miles

❺ Shortly after the pub, on your left there is a concrete track, marked 'The Ridge' on OS maps. You can take a short cut across the bay here at low tide, though it is slippery in places. Otherwise walk all the way round the bay, keeping the water on your left. Head east on a quiet lane, to the second track on the left after the lodge.
1.2 miles

❻ Go up the track, which joins a lane next to a house on the right, walk uphill on the lane until you reach a junction. Turn left here, walk along the road then look out for a footpath leading into fields on your right.
0.7 miles

❼ Cross two fields, keeping to the right boundary in the first, and the centre in the second. You'll then reach a small valley with a path running down it towards the sea. This isn't marked as a right of way on the map but in reality it is commonly used. Once at the coast, turn left on the coast path and retrace your earlier steps to return to the car park.
1 mile

Walk 5

CLEDDAU AT LLAWHADEN

Explore the peaceful Pembrokeshire countryside on this river valley walk through woodland and meadows and with an impressive medieval castle standing high over the river Cleddau.

INFORMATION

Mostly following good tracks and paths through woodland and fields, but there is a short section of a road with no pavement, and a steep set of steps. Expect mud and slippery slopes in places.

DISTANCE: 6 miles
TIME: Walking time 3 hours, not including swimming or visiting the castle.
MAP: OS Explorer OL36 South Pembrokeshire
START & END POINT: Llawhaden Green (SN 070 174, SA67 8HN). Dedicated parking area for several cars.
PUBLIC TRANSPORT: Trains stop at Clunderwen, 2 miles from the route. Bus 381, Haverfordwest to Tenby, stops at Canaston Bridge, from where you can follow the Landsker Borderlands trail for 2 miles to reach Llawhaden.
SWIMMING: Cleddau river at Gelli Bridge (SN 085 197) and several spots further downstream (SN 079 184)
PLACES OF INTEREST: Llawhaden Castle, Llawhaden Bridge ancient monument
REFRESHMENTS: None on the route but head to nearby Narberth for some of the best food options in Pembrokeshire. Try Madtom (SA67 7AT, 01834 860506) for pub favourites. Stock up for a picnic at Wisebuys (SA67 7AR, 01834 861880) or pop in to vegetarian café Plum Vanilla Café (SA67 7DB, 01834 862762). For the ultimate taste of Pembrokeshire book ahead to treat yourself to a very special wild food ten-course tasting menu at Annwn (SA67 7AU, 07308 313107).

Llawhaden is an attractive and peaceful village, set on a hill above the Eastern Cleddau river, deep in the Pembrokeshire countryside. A quiet milieu today, in years gone by it was anything but. The surrounding hills were home to defensive forts, with excavations revealing the highest concentration anywhere in West Wales of defensive structures from the Bronze Age through to the Iron Age. Traces of Roman road have been found nearby in recent years, outside the previously accepted westernmost extent of Roman occupation, Carmarthen. An early chapel is thought to have been established on the banks of the river here by St Aidan, and 10th century references name Llawhaden as one of seven 'Bishop Houses' in the Kingdom of Dyfed. It was certainly considered an important enough site for the first Norman Bishop of St Davids to construct a fortified residence here in the early 12th century.

Our walk begins from the green on the hilltop at Llawhaden and follows a quiet lane along to the castle. The first castle here was likely constructed of timber and earth for Bishop Bernard, perhaps on the site of an earlier hillfort. This structure was destroyed by the native Welsh some 80 years after it had been built. The castle which remains is more of a fortified palatial mansion than a true castle, and was built for Bishop Bek in the 14th century, who used it when travelling around the diocese and for hosting important visitors and pilgrims. The surrounding town was populated by English settlers and became one of the largest towns in south-west Wales, with a weekly market, annual fairs and a hospital for the sick and infirm. The town became an important stop on the westbound pilgrimage route to St David's. It is well

worth spending some time exploring the castle's spectacular gatehouse, apartment buildings and outer walls with battlements you can climb for a wonderful view over the surrounding countryside.

Continuing away from the castle, there is an enjoyable descent through a sloping meadow emerging at the farm, fishery and stables at Holgan ❷. From here the walk enters woodland in a steep-sided valley and, although not accessible, the hilltop above holds the remains of an extensive oval ditch-and-bank enclosure which was occupied for at least four centuries from the 2nd century BC to the 2nd century AD.

The walk is easy going and enjoyable, with birdsong filling the canopy; listen out for the high-pitched trill of goldcrests, the twittering of long-tailed tits, and the cries of fledgling buzzards and red kites calling from their treetop nests to their parents soaring out over the valley. The trees are a mixture of plantation conifers and deciduous native species. ❸ The path winds around the hillsides, keeping more or less on an even contour, before descending and eventually emerging on a quiet lane ❹, where it meets the Syfynwy river just before its confluence with the Eastern Cleddau river at Gelli.

Gelli is a small settlement which during the 19th century had a woollen mill, attracting workers to the area and growing the population. Today nothing remains of the mill, it having been destroyed in a fire in the early 20th century.

Here the river is humble in its earlier stages, flowing from its source near the Preseli Mountains. Along with the Western Cleddau, this is one of the westernmost rivers in Britain. The two combine to become Daugleddau, a tidal river and estuary, flowing past Pembroke Dock into the deep Milford Haven waterway. The river has an important population of otters, and key fish species such as bullhead and lamprey. Salmon and sea trout are also found in the river.

At the old stone bridge at Gelli, there is a first opportunity to swim. The western bank is private for fishing, but on the opposite side there is a pleasant open grassy area with picnic tables. It's a great spot for lunch, and has a bank from which you can ease your way down into the pool in the river for a wonderfully relaxed swim. Do make sure you are confident of getting out the same way before you go down, and don't swim if there are anglers present. As always, make sure you have checked and cleaned your swimming gear from previous swims and are not wearing skin lotions or cosmetics before entering this environment, part of

the Cleddau Rivers Special Area of Conservation, and tread lightly.

Continuing on the lane, there is a steep climb uphill on a minor road, and one on which motorists tend to drive very quickly. There is no pavement, so do take care on this section. It is over soon enough and you'll find yourself back in the fields ❺, with wonderful views across the valley back towards Llawhaden Castle on the hilltop. This is part of the Landsker Borderlands Trail, a 58-mile signposted long-distance route through the Pembrokeshire and Carmarthenshire countryside, exploring the Landsker Line, a historic linguistic and cultural frontier which divides the historically more Anglicised and Welsh parts of Pembrokeshire.

The route drops down into woodland, then reaches the river again ❻. There are several spots along this stretch where you might want to go in for a dip, the best perhaps being on a bend in the river opposite a farm, where there is a deep pool and stony beach for an easy entry and exit into the water. In normal conditions it is wonderful to swim a short distance against the flow and float back down enjoying the gentle pull of the current.

After entering woods again, the path emerges in fields on the opposite side of the river to the church which, rebuilt in the 19th century, sits on the site of an earlier Celtic dedication to St David, mentioned in an early medieval poem. There is an interesting and unusual double tower and an early medieval incised cross, part of which is now housed in the Scolton Museum in Haverfordwest.

Soon after leaving the field ❼, you will reach Llawhaden Bridge, an ancient monument which once marked the lowest crossing point of the river. It was rebuilt in the 17th century when the Skyrme family rebuilt the medieval town which was in sharp economic decline, modernising several of the farms and buildings such as the corn mill. The bridge itself is impressive, a Grade II Listed, stone-arched construction. If you would like to explore the river a little further, the path continues downstream. However, to finish there is a steep climb on a track shortly after crossing the river, which would return you directly to the green and the end of the walk.

DIRECTIONS

❶ From the green, head east along a quiet lane past houses to the castle. Go through the gateway if you want to explore the castle then, when returning, turn right in front of the house, next to the castle walls. Turn left before the castle walls if you don't want to go into the castle. Walk alongside the house then take the middle pathway, through trees and a gate. Stick to the right boundary, cross over a track and continue downhill. The gate in the fence at the end of the bottom field is somewhat hidden behind a group of huge trees. Go through the gate to the farm track.
0.5 miles

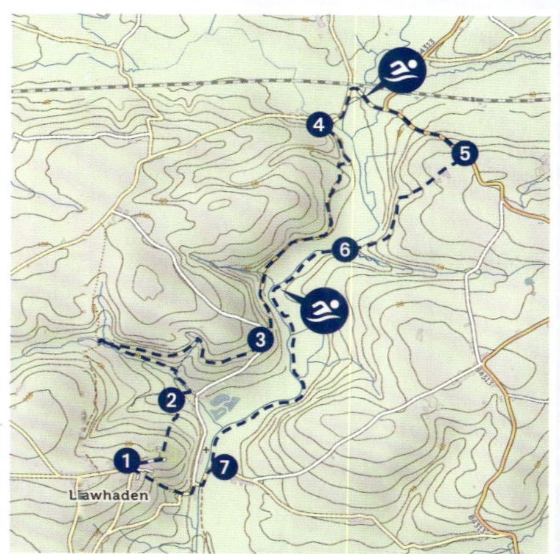

❷ Pass the farm and go through the small gate on the right into the trees. Turn left on the path and go over the footbridge. Stick to the main path through the woods, and just before a gate take a sharp right, almost back on yourself, but heading uphill. At the junction of large tracks, turn right on a forest track (turning left will take you up towards the fort) and continue until you reach a junction with a lane.
1.2 miles

❸ Upon reaching a lane out of the woods, cross over to the middle track, ignoring the turnings onto the lane. Continue down to a farmhouse, and walk through the centre of the barns. Continue on the track and take the left fork through a gate. Follow the track round as it curves left then right. Emerge onto a lane.
1.2 miles

❹ Turn right, and cross the bridge to the picnic spot on the other side, with a climb down the bank to the river. Afterwards, return to the lane, and follow the road round to the right, ignoring the road which goes under the rail bridge. Continue following the lane as it joins another, more-trafficked road. Follow the road steeply uphill with care. As the road levels out and widens, look for a footpath gate next to a larger gate on your right. It can be a bit overgrown and hidden but your gate is to the right of the field gate.
0.7 miles

❺ Keep to the left side of the field, continue through two fields and at the end of the second field, bear right, away from the gate into the next field, and go downhill to the left-hand corner of the woods. Enter the woods through a gate, turn left and continue through the woods on a good path heading down to the river.
0.6 miles

❻ Follow the river through the field, to a deep pool on the bend. In the corner of this field there is a hidden gate. Go through the next field and a double gate through a field, roughly following the river on your right. Enter another short section of woodland, emerge into fields near the church and then leave the fields via the stile and onto a lane.
1.3 miles

❼ Take a right and continue on the lane, crossing the bridge then turning left. Turn right on to a track at the bend in the road. Climb steeply up the track, ignoring steps leading up to a private house. The track will bring you back out at the green and the end of the walk.
0.4 miles

Walk 6

DALE PENINSULA

The ultimate coastal swim-walk with five swim spots – a tranquil harbour, three sheltered bays, and an exhilarating wave-washed beach. Walk in the steps of Henry Tudor and encounter lighthouses, a shipwreck and a geological wonder.

INFORMATION

Mixed terrain: Expect some mud, sandy paths, rocks and grassy clifftops. Steep slopes and steps.

DISTANCE: 7 miles
TIME: 3 hours not including swims
MAP: OS Explorer OL35 South Pembrokeshire
START & END POINT: Dale Harbour (SM 812 058, SA62 3RB)
PUBLIC TRANSPORT: The Fflecsi Milford Haven zone bus connects Dale with Milford Haven and Haverfordwest for the train, as well as other nearby villages.
SWIMMING: Dale Harbour (SM 812 057), Castlebeach Bay (SM 818 051), Watwick Bay (SM 817 040), Mill Bay (SM 809 035), West Dale Bay (SM 798 058).
PLACES OF INTEREST: Dale Fort, Henry Tudor's landing beach at Mill Bay, West Blockhouse, St Ann's lighthouse, Cobbler's Hole geological fold, Great Castle Head Dale Castle
REFRESHMENTS: The Griffin Inn (01646 636227, SA62 3RB), overlooking Dale Harbour, is an award-winning pub/restaurant serving some of the best seafood around. Lobster & Môr (01437 781959, SA62 3UG) in Little Haven is worth the journey for fresh seafood takeaways. There's also the Boathouse café (SA62 3RB) serving breakfasts, fish and chips, vegetarian food, cakes and ice creams right on Dale Harbour.

The Dale Peninsula is a protruding finger of land pointing directly south, at the mouth of the Milford Haven waterway. Our walk circumnavigates the peninsula, with a dramatic contrast between the sunny, sheltered bays of the east coast and the wild, rugged, wave-pounded coastline of the western seaboard. The Peninsula is reportedly the sunniest place in Wales, and receives the least rainfall of anywhere in Pembrokeshire so, if other areas are washed out, perhaps try your luck with the Peninsula's special microclimate.

We begin in Dale, at the harbour. This spot is well sheltered by Dale Point to the south, and is popular with sailing boats and for other water sports. The harbour is a wonderful high-tide swim, with deep water accessed from a gently sloping stony beach to the south of the floating jetty. On the north side there's a concrete slipway where beach wheelchairs are available for hire, making this a great easy-access spot. When you are swimming here make yourself visible and stay aware of other water users.

Beneath the surface of the calm water of Dale Roads, as the bay is known, a special project is under way, to restore seagrass meadows to the seabed. Seagrass is an astonishing, yet increasingly scarce plant, the only flowering plant found in the sea, and one which stores carbon at a quicker rate than tropical rainforests. Seagrass provides an important nursery environment for many marine fish species, and can also help improve water quality. Unfortunately, once damaged beyond a certain point, seagrass cannot recover without help, and it is estimated that 92 percent of the seagrass meadows that once covered UK inshore sea beds has been lost.

Dredging, trawling and intense recreational use are particularly damaging. Here in Dale, which has the special qualities needed for seagrass to recover, the Seagrass Project has planted one million seeds over an area of 2 hectares, working with communities and recreational users of the bay to ensure the seagrass is able to thrive.

Leaving Dale behind for now, we take the narrow single-track lane which extends eastwards with tantalising glimpses through the trees of the sea and sail boats. Our path turns south just before reaching the tip of Dale Point, where Dale Fort, a Victorian fort which, along with many other structures around the Milford Haven coastline, was built as part of the nationwide defence against potential French invasion. It is now home to a field studies centre operated since the 1950s by the Field Studies Council, offering courses in environmental education. The 19th-century buildings were constructed on the site of a prehistoric Iron Age fort.

The coast path ❷ winds along fields and descends through trees to a tiny cove, Castlebeach, surrounded by jagged Red Sandstone cliffs. A rocky cove which feels tucked away, it's a lovely sheltered spot for a second swim. Further along the coast path, at the far end of the bay, is Watwick Point Beacon, which acts as a leading light for ships to enter the haven safely.

The next beach, Watwick Bay, lies a short way off the main the coast path and is a little slice of Pembrokeshire paradise. Powdery white sands and turquoise sea lend a subtropical air to the place, and the clarity of the water makes it ideal for snorkelling. It's often very quiet here, and if you want to feel really castaway, you may even be lucky enough – if you go on a weekday outside the school holidays – to have the beach to yourself in summer. Whisper it, but this is a beach to rival Barafundle!

Back on the coast path again ❸ we pass the West Block House which, along with the East Blockhouse across the water on the Angle Peninsula (see Walk 4), was built during the Tudor period to guard the entrance to the Haven because of its strategic importance, subsequently making it a target amid tensions with France.

Our fourth swimming spot, Mill Bay, is another quiet rocky cove, where the Red Sandstone cliffs look spectacular against the blue of the sea and crowned, at many times of year, by bright yellow gorse flowers. Unassuming and quiet it may be, but this beach holds huge significance in British history, for it was here that Henry Tudor, future king of England, came stealthily ashore, having been exiled in France for 14 years. Henry had been born at Pembroke Castle in 1457, descendant of Owen Tudor, of the noble Tudor family of Ynys Môn. He used his Welsh heritage as he marched through Wales, to gain support and forces, meeting little opposition. He travelled all the way to central England where he fought the Battle of Bosworth, during which King Richard III was killed. Henry claimed the throne and founded the Tudor dynasty as Henry VII. Swimming in the serenity of this unassuming bay, it is difficult to conjure up the image of thousands of men coming to land on this tiny tucked-away beach all those centuries ago.

Look carefully amongst the rocks and you'll see the remains of the wreck of HMS Barking which was wrecked here in 1964 while being towed to a wreckers' yard near Swansea. It seems that the ship had other thoughts about its final resting place. Not much remains of the wreck, but do keep an eye out for it when swimming here as some sharp and rusted metal protrudes in places.

Leaving the relative shelter of the western coast of the peninsula behind ❹, we round the

tip at St Ann's Head. There was once a chapel here dedicated to St Ann, and legend says that its construction was ordered by Henry VII, to give thanks for safe passage to Wales. The chapel is said to have had a round tower, and a torch used to be lit on top as a navigational aid. It is one of the oldest lighthouse locations in Wales. The lighthouse today is the only one found on the mainland in Pembrokeshire. The current lighthouse was built in 1844 and automated in 1998.

Just past the lighthouse, a path leads off towards a large cleft in the cliffs known as Cobbler's Hole. There is a spectacular fold in the Old Red Sandstone here, which occurred during the Devonian and Carboniferous geological periods ancient continental plates collided, some 290 to 370 million years ago. It is here too, that our route reaches the western coast of the peninsula **5**, which faces the full force of the open Atlantic Ocean. This is a place to really feel connected to the elements. Thrift, birds-foot-trefoil, sea campion and sheeps' bit flowers adorn the clifftops. Views stretch over the water to Skokholm Island as we head north towards West Dale Bay.

Just before we arrive at the bay, the promontory of Great Castle Head, to the left, bears obvious signs of human constructions. This site was occupied as an Iron Age fort, some of which has been lost to erosion on the seaward side. Evidence has been found here, too, of Roman occupation, and it is also thought to be the very early medieval site of the first Dale castle.

West Dale Bay is accessed down a steep set of steps, leading down to a red-gold-tinged sandy beach, backed by steep and crumbling Red Sandstone cliffs. Thanks to the swell that pounds the shore, this is a popular beach with surfers. There can be strong and unpredictable currents here, so make sure you are confident in your abilities and use careful judgement on where to enter the water. It's an altogether different experience to the beaches on the more sheltered eastern side, and makes a for an exhilaratingly wild splash in the waves.

Leaving the western coast behind **6**, we return inland through the wrist of the peninsula, past Dale Castle, a grand private home built in 1910, incorporating parts of the earlier 13th century castle. A short walk across Dale Meadows, leading back to the harbour, takes us through the marshy grassland. It's a great place for spotting birds; we came across a snipe and lots of goldfinch here. Just around the coast to the north, though not on our route, there's even better birdwatching at the Pickleridge shingle bank and brackish pools known as the Gann. Head back to Dale for a post-walk drink or bite to eat.

DIRECTIONS

1 After a swim in the harbour, follow the lane past the houses into the trees to the south of the harbour, with the sea on your left. Continue on the lane until just before the entrance to the field studies centre, where you'll see a path into fields on the right, signposted for the Wales Coast Path.
0.8 miles

2 Take the footpath and follow it around the field and down into a small wooded valley. Turn left here to get on to Castlebeach for another swim. Return to the coast path and continue walking along fields, going through a gate on your left to go into the valley ahead. Keep an eye out for the path on your left descending to Watwick Bay, the third swim opportunity.
1.4 miles

3 Climb back up to the main coast path and turn left. Skirt along the hillside with the sea always to your left. Round the point at West Blockhouse Fort, and continue on the path heading west, until it curves around next to Mill Bay. Descend over the rocks here for another swim.
1.1 miles

4 Return to the path and turn left. As you approach the houses ahead, keep left, then continue straight ahead to reach the lighthouse. Follow the lane north-west and, just after the round building, look for a small path along the fence heading towards the sea if you want to visit the Cobbler's Hole rock formation. Return to the lane, pass the old lighthouse and reach the parking area near the houses.
0.7 miles

5 Take the footpath on the left, and follow it keeping close to the coast, with fields to your right, until you reach the top of West Dale Bay; descend on the steps to reach the beach.
2.3 miles

6 Return to the top of the steps then take the first path inland heading towards the castle. Join the lane after passing the castle and head east. Take the track on the right into the car park then, on the other side of the car park, turn right to return to the harbour.
0.8 miles

Walk 7

MARLOES PENINSULA

A clifftop walk around the Marloes Peninsula bestowed with sweeping edge-of-the-world views out over the sea to the islands of Skokholm and Skomer, plunging cliffs, golden sandy tidal bays with crystal clear water and plenty of wildlife spotting opportunities.

The journey out to Marloes follows winding lanes lined in wild flowers, to one of the far western reaches of Pembrokeshire, so that you feel miles away from it all before you even start to walk. Marloes village is small with just a church, village shop, pub and hall. In years gone by, the main livelihoods were farming and fishing: lobster and crab in particular. The locals, traditionally nicknamed 'gulls' referring to their past practice of harvesting gulls' eggs from the offshore islands, also used to make a living selling leeches from the water at Marloes Mere. The village has been English-speaking for 900 years.

The walk begins from the Marloes Sands National Trust car park where there are facilities and a fantastic café. A good track leads down to our first swim spot of the day, the spectacular Marloes Sands. Here the golden sand is interspersed by jagged rocks and vertiginous cliffs. Consisting of a range of rocks from the Silurian period, including volcanic rocks and sandstone, some contain fossilised ripples, from when they were formed in a shallow lagoon some 440 million years ago.

The water here is crystalline and emerald green, with waves foaming onto the shore. Take care of submerged rocks during less calm conditions, but during still spells it's possible to snorkel around the rocks or go for a longer swim across the bay and explore the kelp beds. Swimming here is best at mid- to low-tide, as the rocks at the top of the beach would make for trickier entry and exit at the highest tide. It's also possible to become cut off by

INFORMATION

Mixed terrain: expect some mud, sandy paths, rocks and grassy clifftops. Some easy rock scrambling and steep slopes and steps. Beach access is tide-dependent. Toilets at the start next to the Runwayskiln Café and at Martin's Haven, half way.

DISTANCE: 5½ miles
TIME: 3 hours not including swims
MAP: OS Explorer OL36 South Pembrokeshire
START & END POINT: Marloes Sands National Trust car park (SM 779 083, SA62 3BH)
PUBLIC TRANSPORT: The Flecsi bus service covers this area; at time of writing this was available 6 days a week, not including Sundays. It links with the train at Haverfordwest and Milford Haven.
SWIMMING: Marloes Sands (SM 781 076), Martin's Haven (SM 761 092) and Musselwick Sands (SM 785 090)
PLACES OF INTEREST: Albion Sands shipwreck, Iron Age fort, inscribed stone, Marloes Beacon
REFRESHMENTS: The Runwayskiln (SA62 3BH, 01646 636545) is a fantastic café with great coffee, cakes, brunch and seasonal dishes. You can pick up drinks and snacks en route in the Wildlife Trust visitor centre at Lockley Lodge, open seasonally (SM 761 089, 01646 636800). Otherwise head into Marloes to The Lobster Pot Inn for pub food (SA62 3AZ, 01646 636233).

the tide if you wander along the beach, so do stay aware of what the tide is doing.

It would be easy to spend an entire day here, but the walk ahead is very much worth dragging yourself away for. Climb steeply up the coast path heading ever west ❷, and the expansive views over the open ocean are spectacular, glittering on a summer afternoon, with islands dotted offshore. The cliff path skirts above the beach and gives a birds-eye perspective over the turquoise water and sands below.

Offshore to the south-west is the island of Skokholm, an island seabird sanctuary owned and managed by the Wildlife Trust of South and West Wales. Smaller than its larger and more famous neighbour Skomer, Skokholm is nonetheless an important colony for seabirds including puffins, razorbills, Manx shearwater, storm petrels and gulls.

Closer to shore there's an island, almost joined to the mainland, which dominates the far end of the bay, nearing as you continue on the coast path; this is Gateholm Island. The path reaches a crux here, with steep cliffs and the beach of Albion Sands below. The beach was named after the wreck of the Albion, a paddle steamer travelling from Ireland in April of 1837, which struck a rock as it passed through Jack Sound, the notoriously dangerous stretch of water you can see ahead of you between the mainland and the offshore islands. The ship was stricken and turned onto its side. Somehow it righted itself but, fatally damaged and taking on water, she landed onto what is now known as Albion Sands. All 180 passengers and crew, plus pigs, horses and other goods were saved. A sale of the salvaged items was held directly on the beach. Remains of the wreck still rest in the sands.

As the path turns north-west, it skirts the cliff edge with staggering drops and rocks jutting out into the sea. The remains of earthworks from an Iron Age fort are visible; the route takes you right through the centre of where the fort would have been – part of it has perhaps been lost to the sea due to cliff erosion.

Continuing along the cliffs, your eyes will be drawn over to Skomer Island and the smaller Midland Isle which lies between the mainland and Skomer. The water of Jack Sound is an excellent place to spot porpoises feeding in the turbulent currents. This entire area, including Skokholm is a Special Protected Area, a designation for the protection of the internationally important colonies of seabirds that can be found here. Although the puffins are undoubtedly what draw the majority of visitors to the island, Skomer has around 350,000 pairs of Manx shearwaters. Along with Skokholm this is the largest breeding population in the world. Skomer and the surrounding waters were also Wales' first Marine Conservation Zone, designated in 2014, to protect a number of species, including grey seals and various seabed organisms. For this reason, certain fishing practices such as dredging and trawling are prohibited.

The route reaches a small valley running north-south, with a headland to the west. The two are separated by a large stone wall, the legacy of an attempt to construct a deer park here in the 18th century – one which never came to fruition. The area is still known as the Deer Park despite there never having been any deer here! You could extend the walk here if you wanted, by simply following the coastline around the headland for fantastic views over Jack Sound. If you are unable to visit any of the offshore islands, the walk around the headland is the next best thing. In autumn, seals can be seen in the inaccessible coves below.

❸ If you're short on time or just want to get on for another swim, don't enter the deer park but instead head directly north towards Martin's Haven. This rocky cove is where boats depart for the islands; tickets sell out months in advance for peak season, but during the shoulder seasons you may be lucky if you arrive early and call into Lockley Lodge just above the cove, where you can also find refreshments. A small information centre and toilet block is on the left as you near the beach. Note the stone cross set into the wall, dated 9th-10th century and thought to be a prayer stone for travellers to the islands.

If you're planning to swim, remember that the cove can be busy through the spring and summer, with boats coming in and out to ferry passengers to Skomer and Skokholm. Boat traffic is generally on the left as you look out to sea, where there is a jetty; it would be a good idea to wear a brightly coloured swim cap and tow float here, and stick to the right-hand side of the cove, which is excellent for snorkelling and popular with scuba divers. Be aware of seals in residence during late summer and autumn, and avoid entering the water or going onto the beach if they are present.

Leaving the haven behind, climb up steeply on the coast path to regain the clifftop, where you'll have a wonderful cruise along the southern coast of St Brides Bay, with views over to Ramsey Island and Solva. Before long the tantalisingly golden sands of Musselwick Bay come into view and you'll scarcely be able to get there quickly enough! A narrow path takes you down from the main coast path to a huge swathe of smoothly sculpted cliff with steps cut into the stone. Although confident swimmers can access the water here at high tide in calm conditions, if you want to enjoy the beach too, time your visit with the outgoing tide. This is a local's favourite and despite the remote setting, on a summer day there will be a few adventurous families out here enjoying the sand and sparkling water. Make sure you plan for enough time here as it really is a special spot and you won't want to leave in a hurry. Once time or tide call you away, ❹ a footpath alongside fields with spectacular views over the coastline takes you back uphill where you'll finish with just less than a mile walking along a minor lane ❺. Before you reach the end of the route, a quick diversion up to the trig point known as Marloes Beacon is well worth it for the panoramic views.

DIRECTIONS

❶ From the entrance of Marloes Sands car park (Runwayskiln side as opposed to Trehill Farm side) take the lane straight ahead, eastwards. Then look for a track on your right heading gently downhill. Turn right at the bottom to follow the path down to Marloes Sands.

0.6 miles

❷ Return to the path and follow the coast path west, keeping the sea to your left. Continue along the path as it follows the cliff edge, all the way to the stone wall next to a house, where the Deer Park begins. Go through the gate to the other side of the wall. If you wish to extend the walk follow the coastline all the way around the headland. Otherwise follow the stone wall north and go through the gate to the other side. Rejoin the route at this point if you have extended it.

2 miles

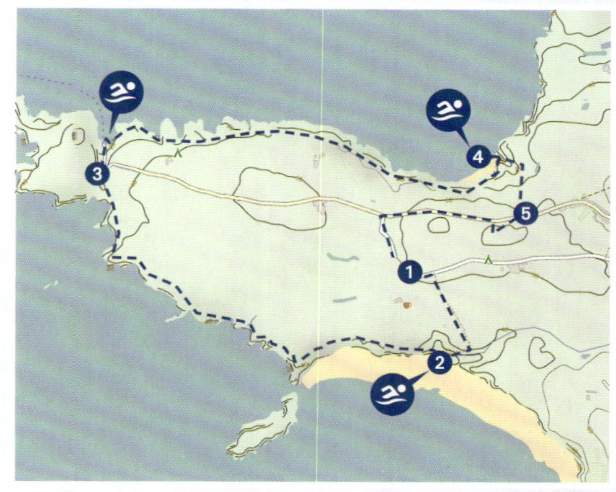

❸ Follow the lane north to reach Martin's Haven. After swimming, climb up the steps on the coast path heading north, then east. Continue with the sea on your left and fields on your right until the path veers northwards. Heading into a valley with a small stream at the base, leave the coast path, following a minor path towards the sea. Climb down over the rocks to reach the beach (low tide only).

2 miles

❹ Return up from the beach the same way, and where our path crosses the coast path, instead continue ahead on the route leading inland. Follow the path as it turns right and climbs alongside the fields, emerging onto a minor lane.

0.4 miles

❺ Turn right on the lane and walk along it heading west. After a short distance you'll see the Marloes Beacon on the left, for a quick diversion. Otherwise continue along the lane until you reach the entrance to a lane in front of the house on the left. Turn into the lane, which enters the Marloes Sands car park from the opposite end.

0.7 miles

Walk 8

SOLVA

A beguiling route offering a real variety of swims, from deep harbour water to hidden coves. Explore traditional countryside with hidden history and climb to the clifftops for staggering views.

As you arrive in Solva you'll immediately feel welcomed by the colourful stone houses lining the road and the boats bobbing in the picturesque harbour. A stream wends its way among the houses, and gidels – passageways that in years past allowed access to the river for washing clothes and disposing of waste – run between the houses. Italian prisoners of war installed sewage pipes in the 1940s, removing the need for residents to use the river, thankfully for us swimmers. But the main street gidel has been restored allowing you to see how they would have been. The village has gift and antique shops, galleries, a pottery, fresh seafood outlets, and several pubs and cafés, so is very popular with visitors and makes an excellent place to begin and end a walk.

Time your walk so that you'll be able either to end or begin at high tide, when the harbour is full. At low tide the water in the harbour drains out completely and the boats are left resting on the sand. There are two jetties where you can get into the water. The furthest right at the end of the quay, near the Solva Rowing and Watersports and Sailing Clubs, is best for getting into and out of the deep water. An early morning or evening swim here is wonderfully peaceful. Do be aware of boats coming and going, and respect the club members when they are using the jetty. It is a popular place for swimming with a couple of social swimming groups, the Bluetits and the Solva Swimmers, regularly meeting here. There are also several events here throughout the year; the annual Solva Sailing club regatta and raft race has been held here for 130 years. This includes a hilarious blindfold inflatable dinghy race as well as more serious options, including swims. At the

INFORMATION

You'll encounter every type of terrain on this walk! Expect steep steps and slopes, cliffside paths, stony and sandy coves and a few stiles to cross.

DISTANCE: 5 miles
TIME: 2 hours, not including swims
MAP: OS Explorer OL35 North Pembrokeshire
START & END POINT: Solva Harbour car park (SM 806 243, SA62 6UT)
PUBLIC TRANSPORT: The T11 Trawscymru bus connects Solva directly with Haverfordwest for the train, and with Goodwick for the train and even a ferry to Ireland if needed!
SWIMMING: Solva Harbour (SM 801 241), Porthmynawyd (SM 827 229) and Porth Gwadn (SM 803 224)
PLACES OF INTEREST: Harbour limekilns, Gribin Iron Age fort, St Elvis Neolithic burial chambers
REFRESHMENTS: You're spoilt for choice in Solva! The Harbour Inn (SA62 6UT, 01437 720013), The Ship Inn (SA62 6UU, 01437 721528) and The Cambrian Inn (SA62 6UU, 01437 721210) offer hearty pub meals. The Cambrian Inn is perhaps the more upmarket and gastro of the three, and The Ship the more traditional. Solva is famous for its seafood and both the highly rated Mrs Will the Fish (SA62 6TN, 01437 721571) in the upper town and Something Fishy (SA62 6XJ, 01437 454986) on the road out of the town to Newgale offers fresh takeaway dressed lobster, crab and seafood platters – perfect to pick up and sit by the harbour to enjoy.

beginning of the last century water polo was played as part of the regatta. As part of the local 'Swim to the Edge' series, the Green Monster swim event begins in the harbour and involves a 2-mile swim, out of the harbour and around the Green Scar rock offshore; quite an undertaking! All in all, Solva's harbour is a hive of water activity where recreation is well established and refreshingly celebrated. For that reason, during peak times it can get very busy so parking becomes more of a challenge and an early arrival is recommended.

Being such a sheltered harbour, it is little surprise to know that Solva has a long maritime history. As it was at one time the main shipping port for St Bride's Bay, limestone was imported in large quantities, to be used to improve soil in the surrounding farmland and in buildings. The remains of four large limekilns can be seen alongside the harbour close to the village. In turn, corn was exported from here to other parts of Wales. Culm, a type of coal used to heat the houses, was also imported on flat-bottomed boats. In the 1830s local man Edward Callaghan created a rival business using donkeys to bring culm to the village from Newgale, racing to make his sales before the boats arrived. In the 1840s it was even possible to buy passage to America from Solva, a journey that lasted around 17 weeks and cost £3 (about £300 in today's prices). Shipping, however, was as dangerous a business here as anywhere: in January 1773 the ship Phoebe and Peggy, having sailed all the way from Philadelphia, was wrecked during a severe gale on the St Elvis Rock just outside the harbour. A rescue boat went out from Solva but also got into difficulty and 60 people, including passengers, crew and rescue boatmen, were all tragically lost.

In the 1770s a lighthouse was constructed in the harbour and floated 22 miles out to sea to be installed on rocks known as The Smalls. Although the mission to install the lighthouse was successful, a later tragedy would change how lighthouses were operated forever. In 1801 two lighthouse keepers, Thomas Howell and Thomas Griffith, were out manning the lighthouse when one of them died in an accident. Because the men were known to argue frequently, Howell feared that he would be accused of murder and so did not dispose of Griffith's body. He fashioned a coffin, and strapped it to the outside of the lighthouse but a storm ripped the coffin apart and exposed an arm, left flailing in the wind, seemingly taunting and haunting Howell. It was weeks before anyone arrived to relieve Howell, by which time he was a shadow of his former self and changed forever. From that incident on, all offshore lighthouses across the UK were manned by a minimum of three men and it remained that way until automation. The Smalls Lighthouse, the first to be powered by wind and solar power, has a lamp that can be seen up to 21 miles away, its light not quite visible from Solva.

After a first swim in the harbour, or to begin the walk straight away, the route takes you onto the headland above the harbour ❷; it's named the Gribin, Welsh for Ridge. The ridge was formed from a harder volcanic band of rock, resisting erosion by the rivers on either side. These are, of course, now much smaller than when they were serious glacial meltwater rivers. The views from the top out to sea are spectacular and, as is the case for so many of the prominent headlands along the Pembrokeshire coast, it was also in the Iron Age the location of a fort. Large platforms at the top of the ridge are thought to have held several dwellings and a timber enclosure, while at the end of the ridge there are remains of another settlement overlooking the harbour entrance.

The route descends from the Gribin then crosses the valley ❸, climbing again through woodland and fields towards St Elvis Farm, where there once stood a church dedicated to St Elvis (St Ailfyw in Welsh), who baptised St David. If you wish to take a short detour from our route you can see the much-disturbed but still impressive remains of Neolithic burial chambers close by. ❹ Rejoining the route through fields, away from the farm, pass along a lane, a hedgerow-lined track and then emerge within sight of the coast.

A descent through trees ❺ leads to a path winding through a narrow valley, to a hidden cove named Porthmynawyd. Surrounded by high cliffs on all sides, with gold sand at low tide, this is a wonderfully quiet spot to sunbathe, snorkel, explore the caves, and swim across the bay. At high tide you can coasteer round the rocks to jump in. Seals often take shelter in the bay, but the small beach at high tide leaves them easily disturbed by walkers and dogs so they don't often successfully breed here. Take care not to disturb any that may be in residence during your visit.

❻ There is a steep climb up from the beach and a narrow path out to Dinas Fach headland where there are remains of yet another Iron Age fort. A walk along here offers wonderful views back down to the beach and out across St Brides Bay towards Skomer Island. From here a spectacular section of coast path follows the cliff edge back towards Solva, but not before a final treat for the day, a swim at the lovely Gwadn beach. A local's favourite, this gorgeous sheltered spot is perfect for a swim or snorkel, although it can be quite shallow at low tide. For more adventurous swimmers at high tide, you could feasibly swim from here back round to the slipway in the harbour; take a tow float and wear a bright coloured swim hat to make sure you're visible to boats. ❼ Otherwise, there is a final steep climb back up onto the Gribin and down the other side through trees to return to the village.

DIRECTIONS

1 From the harbour car park, walk down the harbour side on the coast path. You will pass a jetty to access the water, or continue until you reach the sailing club and café buildings. There is a coast path sign leading to steep steps, which is as far as you want to go. The jetty here is a good place to access the water if the clubs aren't using it. After swimming retrace your steps to the harbour car park and cross the bridge over the river near the pub.
0.7 miles

2 Once you've crossed the bridge, take a path on your left, climbing uphill, then switching back through the trees to emerge at the top of the Gribin. Turn left, inland, then go through the gate on your right to zigzag downhill to the valley. Go past the waterworks building, cross the bridge and then uphill south-east up through trees.
0.4 miles

3 When you emerge from the trees, there is a junction in the path with a fingerpost at the top. Turn left, then follow the path through the fields to St Elvis Farm. A short detour down a path leading south-west will take you to the burial chambers. Otherwise continue on a narrow path south-west through fields until you reach a lane at Lochvane Farm.
0.8 miles

4 Continue on the lane through the buildings and you'll see a path leading off to your right between tall hedgerows. At the end of the hedgerows cross into a field and turn left, following the path around the perimeter of the field with the fence on your left to find a stile into the trees in the bottom south-eastern corner of the field.
0.5 miles

5 Walk through the trees downhill then turn right and continue downhill. You'll cross the coast path but continue ahead through the valley to reach the beach.
0.2 miles

6 Return to the coast path and turn left climbing steeply uphill. Follow the coast path keeping the sea on your left until you reach a gate above Gwadn Cove. Descend steeply to reach the cove.
2 miles

7 On the far side of the beach cross the bridge over the stream then take the very steep path uphill back on to the end of the Gribin. There is a jumble of paths here but continue north-west on the coast path, descending through trees to reach the bridge to cross back over to Solva harbour car park.
0.5 miles

Walk 9

ST NON'S AND ST DAVIDS

St Davids is a city of religious and natural reverence, where people are drawn either to pray, or play in the wild blue waters encompassing the peninsula. This walk offers some adventurous swims and explorations of the rocky coves in the birthplace of coasteering, with an insight into the fascinating spiritual history of this place of pilgrimage along the way.

INFORMATION

Mixed terrain: well-trodden coast path, steps and steep climbs, country lanes. Access to the sea at St Non's and Ogof Golchfa requires a steep climb down and some rock scrambling. Toilets and water refill at Porthclais, halfway.

DISTANCE: 5½ miles
TIME: 3 hours not including swims
MAP: OS Explorer OL35 North Pembrokeshire
START & END POINT: St Davids Cathedral car park and bus stop (SM 750 253, SA62 6PS)
PUBLIC TRANSPORT: To reach St Davids take the T11 bus from Haverfordwest or Fishguard with train and even ferry connections. Out of season use the Fflecsi on-demand transport service (tfw.wales/fflecsi). The 403 Celtic Coaster bus service runs between Tydewi / St Davids and Porthclais during summer.
SWIMMING: Coasteering at St Non's bay (SM 751 242) Sheltered harbour swimming at Porthclais (SM 741 242), tidal pools & rocky inlet at Ogof Golchfa (SM 741 237), and remote cove at Porthlysgi (SM 731 238).
PLACES OF INTEREST: St Davids Cathedral and Bishop's Palace, St Non's Chapel and Well, Picrite boulder, Clegyr Boia settlement.
REFRESHMENTS: There's a fantastic kiosk at Porthclais harbour which is great for mid walk refreshments and snacks. (SA62 6RR). Otherwise, there are many options in St Davids (see Carn Llidi and St Davids Head chapter).

Tyddewi, St Davids, is famous as the birthplace of Wales' patron saint, Dewi or David. According to legend, his mother, St Non, gave birth to him on a clifftop during a violent storm. He grew to become a monk, travelling widely as a preacher, and established a monastery in the sheltered valley of the river Alun, where our walk begins.

St David reportedly performed many miracles during his lifetime. The most well-known was during a sermon in the village of Llanddewi Brefi, where people who stood at the back of the crowd that had gathered to listen to his sermon complained that they couldn't hear him. The ground he was standing on rose miraculously, and a white dove came to settle on his shoulder, as a sign of blessing from God. He lived an austere and simple life, as a vegetarian who drank only water, keeping bees and ploughing the land for growing. He could often be found standing neck-deep in the sea reciting psalms as penance. I wonder what he would make of those of us today who can often be found neck-deep in the sea for pleasure! David's final words to his followers were 'Gwnewch y pethau bechan mewn bywyd', 'Do the little things in life'.

The cult of St David continued to grow after his death at the end of the 6th century, and the monastery continued to be used despite repeated attacks from Viking raiders. In 1081, William the

Conqueror famously visited St Davids to pray. In the early 12th century, King Henry I appointed a bishop to head of the Cathedral. And, shortly afterwards, Pope Calixtus II named St Davids as a Place of Pilgrimage, meaning that two pilgrimages to St Davids equalled one to Rome.

Today, St Davids, the smallest city in Britain, is as much a place of pilgrimage for lovers of the outdoors and coastal wildness, as it is for spiritual pilgrims. The entire peninsula is of stunning beauty, with unmatched coastline, wildlife, walking trails and adventure activities, making it a hugely popular destination for visitors.

Our route today begins in the centre of St Davids, and heads out to the coast along a quiet country lane. We reach the sea at the ruined St Non's Chapel and Holy Well. Set on the clifftop where St David was reportedly born, the well is said to have sprung up at the moment of his birth. The views here out over St Brides Bay with Skomer Island visible on the horizon, and the sparkling azure waters lapping the cliffs below, are something to behold. If you're not moved by the spiritual history, you certainly won't fail to be taken by the natural beauty of this place.

❷ A steep scramble from the coast path takes us down to the rocky St Non's Bay. Not only the birthplace of a patron saint, this special place is also known as the birthplace of coasteering! In the 1980s, owners of an eco-lodge in the area coined the term for this now much-loved adventure activity which involves scrambling around rocks on the coast and jumping into the sea, exploring caves and getting thrashed about by waves. It's great fun and if you're inexperienced or want to explore harder-to-reach areas then there are a multitude of companies offering coasteering here and in the wider area that can fit you up with helmets, buoyancy aids, wetsuits and expert guiding.

St Non's Bay is perfect on a calm day for snorkelling amongst kelp and rocks and swimming through a cave arch at the eastern side. A tow float and brightly coloured swim cap will keep you visible to other water users; kayaking groups also love it here. A wetsuit and footwear with grip will also help protect you and your feet on the sharp and slippery rocks.

❸ Continuing along the coast path, we reach the pretty harbour of Porthclais. Once used to land goods to supply the cathedral and Bishops' Palace, and thought to have been used even earlier by the Romans, today it is a busy harbour popular with kayaking groups, and used for mooring small fishing and leisure boats. If you want to swim in the harbour then reach it for high tide and stay aware of watercraft around you. Again, make yourself visible with a tow float and bright swim cap. At low tide you can scramble down outside the harbour wall and swim in the deeper water there.

❹ Back on the coast path, after rounding the western edge of the harbour, you can descend a grassy slope onto the rocks to explore tidal pools and a small hidden inlet known as Ogof Golchfa, Washing Cave! As the name may suggest, you need calm conditions to explore this part of the coast.

5 Further on, at the south-westernmost tip of our walk, keep a keen eye out for what may seem an unremarkable boulder, but is in fact a Glacial Erratic, thought to have been moved here by glaciers all the way from north-west Wales! The rock type is picrite, and its precise composition is not found in this area. In past times it was thought to have been a meteorite, as meteorites have similar mineral compositions. This rock is considered special enough to be marked on the Ordnance Survey map!

Porth Lysgi comes into view ahead, an enticing cove of fine sand and cut-glass turquoise water. This is a wonderful place for easy swimming, snorkelling and sunbathing and you could spend hours here. Don't be surprised if you're joined by a couple of curious companions bobbing in the bay; a relatively short distance offshore is Ramsey Island, home one of the largest colonies of Atlantic Grey seals in Britain. Around 600 pups are born on the island each year and this part of the mainland coast often sees visiting seals who come to bask in the calm waters of the coves. In the breeding season be sure to keep your distance.

6 Leaving the coast behind, we walk inland to Upper Treginnis to join a quiet lane heading back to St Davids. On your left appears the rocky outcrop of Clegyr Boia, named after renowned Irish pirate Boia, who is believed to have established a settlement there. St David, when establishing his monastery in the valley below Boia's settlement, angered the chieftain, who sent his men to drive David away. David is said to have cast a spell on Boia's cattle, making them appear dead. This led Boia to surrender to David and convert to Christianity. Boia was later said to have died in battle with Irish invader Lisci (whose name is preserved at Porthlysgi).

Evidence of occupation as far back as the Neolithic period has been shown at the outcrop; with remains of pottery and huts dating back at least 5,000 years, a rare surviving example of Neolithic settlement which, unlike their burial chambers, are few in Wales.

7 Our walk continues into the wooded valley and returns to St Davids. Here you'll see the Cathedral, and ruins of the once magnificent Bishop's Palace. These buildings date to the 12th century when Norman Bishop de Leia began construction on the site of St David's earlier monastery. The Cathedral's history has been as vibrant as the purple sandstone from which it was built. In the early 1200s an earthquake caused the tower to collapse. And in the 14th century, Bishop Henry Gower attracted huge donations from noble pilgrims, whom he entertained in his grand palace. The cathedral was ransacked during the Reformation, and many of the shrines and artefacts were lost. Further damage was wreaked during the civil war in the 1400s. Much restoration work has helped preserve the Cathedral during subsequent years, and today the Cathedral is still considered the most important religious site in Wales. It's well worth a visit, along with the ruins of the Bishop's Palace.

DIRECTIONS

❶ From the car park / bus stop south-west of the cathedral, walk uphill then take a short cut-through footpath on your right, leading to a lane. Continue straight ahead, southwards, on the lane, climbing gently, then levelling out as you pass the hotel on your right. The lane descends gently and comes to an end at St Non's Retreat. Turn right here into the field and head towards the ruins of St Non's Chapel.
0.7 miles

❷ From the chapel, continue ahead to the coast path, then turn left, heading east. Look for a steep rocky descent for your first swim, to the sea on your right, where there is a faint stream.
0.1 mile

❸ Return to the coast path and continue with the sea to your left until you reach the harbour of Porthclais. There is a steep path down to the harbour wall if you want to swim on the seaward side of it at low tide. Otherwise continue ahead, and wade in from the pebble beach at high tide.
1 mile

❹ Continue on the coast path heading uphill, southwards. As the path makes a 90 degree turn to the right, take the lower path and branch off to the left, heading carefully down the grassy slope then scramble over the rocks to reach the tidal pools and Ogof Golchfa.
0.5 miles

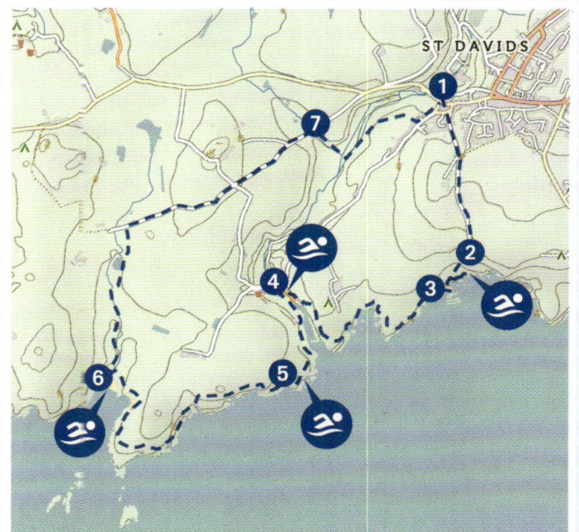

❺ Return to the coast path, follow it keeping the sea to your left, until you reach the shore of Porthlysgi for a final swim.
1.2 miles

❻ From the shore, turn inland heading north on a National Trust path, past the pool at Treginnis Uchaf then to meet the lane. Turn right on the lane and continue until you see a bridlepath sign down a track also signposted for 'Felin Isaf' on your right.
1.3 miles

❼ Take the right down the track, then walk through the buildings at the end, and take a path on the left which follows a stream. Branch off right onto a track, which joins a lane. Turn left on the lane and follow it as it branches left, then left again to return to the start.
0.6 miles

Walk 10

CARN LLIDI AND ST DAVIDS HEAD

Soak up the laidback surf vibes at one of Pembrokeshire's most-loved sandy beaches. Then head off on the coast path to luxuriate in the elysian waters at two quieter sandy coves. Venture onto the rugged headland and climb to the peak of Carn Llidi for edge-of-the-world vistas and fascinating history.

There's something magnetic about the St Davids Peninsula, and particularly St Davids Head and the rocky outcrop of Carn Llidi standing proud over the surrounding farmland and coastline. Nowhere in Wales is there a sweep of golden sand as breathtaking as Porth Mawr (Whitesands). Rocky islands are dotted offshore, framed by dramatic cliffs, and the crystalline water peels into waves that are revered by surfers from across the country. Porth Mawr is home to its own surf lifesaving club, and also hosts national surfing and surf lifesaving competitions. If you fancy giving it a go yourself, there are surf schools and board hire companies which operate right alongside the beach. Splashing in the waves here is great fun, but on calmer days the sea here can be glassy and great for swimming. The beach is lifeguarded during the summer and has toilets, a café, a slipway onto the beach, and beach-accessible wheelchairs for hire.

All of this beauty and the facilities available here do mean that during holidays and summer weekends there are often queues down the lane to the car park and the beach can get very busy. Thankfully it is a huge beach and if you walk past the crowds gathered above the high tide line closest to the car park, and wander along the beach without going too far you will easily find your own spot of serenity. Go early, in the evening, or during a weekday outside of the school holidays if you'd much rather experience this special place at its most peaceful.

INFORMATION

Good beach access at Porthmawr / Whitesands. Rocky coast path with steps and slopes. Scramble down to Porthlleuog. Short rock scramble to get to top of Carn Llidi. Toilets and water refill at start.

DISTANCE: 4½ miles
TIME: 3 hours not including swims
MAP: OS Explorer OL35 North Pembrokeshire
START & END POINT: Porth Mawr / Whitesands car park (SM 735 272, SA62 6PS)
PUBLIC TRANSPORT: The 403 Celtic Coaster bus service runs between Tydewi / St Davids and Porth Mawr / Whitesands during summer. From here you can use the T11 bus to Haverfordwest or Fishguard for train and even ferry connections. Out of season use the Fflecsi on-demand transport service (tfw.wales/fflecsi).
SWIMMING: Sandy beaches at Porth Mawr / Whitesands Bay (SM 733 271), Porthlleuog (SM 732 274) and Porthmelgan (SM 728 279)
PLACES OF INTEREST: Coeten Arthur burial chamber, Clawdd y Milwyr fort, Highwinds submarine listening post, site of St Patrick's Chapel
REFRESHMENTS: There's a café in the car park (SM 735 272, 01437 720168). Otherwise head to St Davids (SA62 6SA). For local produce try the higher-end Y Gegin (07961 290527), The Bishops (01437 720422) for great pub food and a lovely beer garden, Pebbles Yard Gallery (01437 720122) for cakes & coffee, Grain (01437 454321) for wood-fired pizzas and beer in a courtyard.

At sunset on a warm summer's day the beach holds a different kind of magic, with sun glitter on the water and a sorbet sky. You could time your swim either at the beginning of the walk, or return here to coincide with sunset for a swimming experience that will stay with you for a long time.

Although not on our route, it would be amiss not to mention the next cove along to the south, Porthselau. Not only is it another beautiful place to swim, but it is the birthplace of the now-international Bluetits Chill Swimmers. Campsite owner Sian Richardson began winter swimming as a personal challenge and soon others started to join her. Nicknaming themselves the Bluetits, the group has since multiplied across the world, formalised into a social enterprise and has introduced thousands of people to the joys of cold-water swimming.

The second swim spot on our route is separated from Porth Mawr by only a narrow rocky causeway, reached by following a small path off the main coast path. Just before you get to this point, soon after you've joined the coast path from the car park, there is a flat area of dunes to your left. In recent years excavations have been undertaken at this spot by the Dyfed Archaeological Trust, after erosion during severe storms. Their work uncovered more than ninety burials. The site is thought to have been used as a cemetery as far back as the 6th century. Interesting finds include glass and amber beads, along with cross-incised stones.

In calm conditions you can scramble down the lowest part of the Trwynhwrddyn causeway which separates the two beaches to reach Porth Lleuog, to swim or snorkel around the rocks submerged in the bay. The colour of the water is a dazzling emerald and the water is often sheltered. Make sure you are confident you can scramble back up the rocks as there is no other escape from this beach and at high tide the water comes right up to the base of the high cliffs. Avoid this spot during seal pupping season as seal pups are often born in the coves just around the corner.

2 Returning to the coast path, you'll climb high to increasingly expansive views over to Ramsey Island and the Bishops and Clerks islands. These islands were notoriously treacherous for passing vessels and thirteen shipwrecks are recorded here. As a consequence, the South Bishop lighthouse was erected, in 1834 (read more about this in Walk 8 – Solva). The islands are home to small colonies of birds including storm petrels and puffins.

Our path begins to cross the heath and heads onto National Trust land, sometimes frequented by ponies for conservation grazing. Before long the path heads downhill and comes to Porthmelgan, our third swim spot, the picture-perfect golden sandy cove, with a real castaway feeling. Most of the visitors to Porth Mawr don't make it this far, so it is much quieter and a perfect place to swim, explore caves and sunbathe. The beach is accessible at high tide, but better at mid- to low-tide when the sea comes off the rocks onto sand. It is a steep

beach, so can be liable to strong currents, but in generally calm weather it's a sheltered spot. Savour the final swim, then rejoin the path and follow it as it hugs the curve of the headland beyond the beach, lined with gorse and heather. ❸ In late summer the headland is blanketed in a pattern of yellow and purple, the scent of coconut and honey mixing with the salty sea breeze. Butterflies, bees and other insects thrive here, supported by a proliferation of ragwort, yarrow and bird's foot trefoil. Look out for the striking red and black cinnabar moths, which start life as black and yellow caterpillars. Kestrels are often seen hovering above the heath, and there is also a healthy population of adders here. Don't worry though; they're very shy of humans and will likely slither off if you get too close.

As you climb out to the end of the headland, you'll pass through some well-preserved defences of the Clawdd y Milwyr Iron Age fort. The fort is thought to have held eight round houses. The foundations of six of them can still be made out today if you have a keen eye. Continue climbing out as far as you can without tumbling off the edge of the cliff, and taking care in strong winds. Here is a wonderful vantage point with an edge-of-the-world feeling. It's one of the best spots in Pembrokeshire to spot porpoises and seals swimming past, as the current which runs between Ramsey and the mainland and all the way up to Strumble Head to the north provides a feast of fish. Occasionally you may see dolphins passing and, though much rarer, even whales and sharks have been seen in the area. Bring some binoculars and keep your eyes peeled.

❹ Heading north-west from the fort, the path crosses the heathland and passes the huge stone burial chamber known as Coeten Arthur. The four metre by three metre capstone sits on the ground at one side and is supported by a stone at the other end. The chamber is considered to have held a passage grave, from the Neolithic period some 5,000 years ago. It is quite a humbling experience to stand in this spot and consider the lives of the humans that were occupying this land all that time ago.

Our route leaves the coast path and turns inland, past an ancient settlement and field system on the north-western slopes of Carn Llidi. ❺ Climbing alongside an impressive stone wall, when you get to the crest of the slope you have the choice to take an out-and-back diversion to climb to the top of the outcrop. You'll need a head for heights and to be steady on your feet to reach the very top, but it is absolutely worth it for the jaw-dropping panoramic views over the peninsula and out to sea. One memorable evening I climbed up to watch the sun set on the summer solstice. There is an almost spiritual feeling here; Carn Llidi carries a special energy which draws you in, a natural tower to mirror the one at the mighty St Davids cathedral.

❻ Climb down the way you came, rejoining the path to the north east of Carn Llidi, then follow it around to the south, where the views of the islands catch your breath once again, before returning to Whitesands beach.

DIRECTIONS

1 From the beach car park, walk down the slipway to access the beach. Return to the car park then join the coast path at a gap in the wall. After 200 metres take a narrow path left to walk out on to the rocky causeway Trwynhwrddyn. Descend some steps then at the rocky section, find a place to scramble down safely to the right to access Porth Lleuog for a second swim; make sure you can safely scramble back up again.
0.2 miles

2 Return to the coast path and continue heading north-west, following a boundary to your right, until it turns 90 degrees to the north-east. Don't turn to follow the wall here, but keep straight ahead through an area of heathland, and follow the path until it descends to Porthmelgan.
0.6 miles

3 After swimming and exploring the cove, return back to the coast path and turn left, following the path as it curves to the west, skirting the cliffs above the cove. Continue west as far as you can, passing the entrance to the Iron Age fort, and walking up onto the rocks for the view.
0.5 miles

4 Return to the fort entry, then take the coast path which follows the north-western coastline of the headland. The burial chamber is on your right. Keep to the coast path, leaving it only as it begins to descend towards a stone wall, changing direction to walk east to a flat area before a steep climb south-east. Follow the path with the wall to your left, and look out for a small path leading towards the peak of Carn Llidi.
1.5 miles

5 If you want to climb Carn Llidi, turn right and follow the path below some rocky outcrops, keeping to the right until the path nears the peak and becomes steeper. Scramble carefully up the rocks to reach the peak. Return to the main path and the stone wall by retracing your steps.
0.6 miles

6 If rejoining the path, turn right. If you didn't climb up to the peak, continue straight ahead, with the boundary on your left. Ignore a sign and gate which leads to the YHA building. Continue ahead until you reach a gate leading to a track. Follow the track through the houses and onto the lane, turning right to return along the lane to the car park.
1 mile

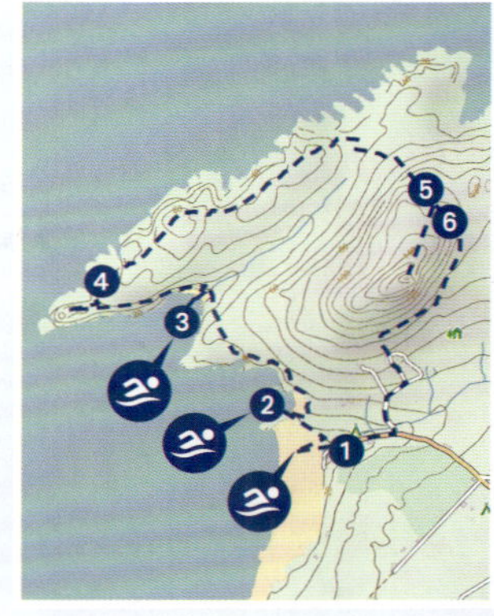

Walk 11

ABEREIDDY AND TREFIN

Walk one of the most spectacular stretches of coast path in Wales. This has a wide variety of swimming options, from exciting jumps to sandy coves with crystal water. Uncover historic coastal industries and wander through classic countryside to coastal hamlets with traditional sailors' pubs.

In contrast to the gentle golden sand beaches further south, the black pebbles and sands of Abereiddy are striking, especially on a blue-sky day when the emerald sea appears exceptionally vibrant. The beach, where this walk begins, is formed from shales dating back to the Ordovician period some 450 million years ago, which have subsequently been eroded by weathering and the sea. With luck you may be able to spot fossils in the rock beds. The most common type here are a type of graptolite referred to as 'tuning fork graptolites', an ancient marine organism whose fossils look a little bit like sycamore seeds.

Conditions at the beach can vary wildly here. In the right conditions it is a popular surf spot, but it can also become very calm and flat too. When swimming be aware of the submerged rock beds, particularly to the left of the beach as you look out to sea.

Despite the raw beauty of the beach, it is not actually the main attraction here. Visitors flock from far and wide to visit the iconic 'Blue Lagoon'. This is an old slate quarry which is flooded by the sea. Minerals from the slate give an exceptionally vibrant green-blue colour to this sheltered pool, wonderful for swimming, kayaking, paddleboarding, and one of the top destinations in Pembrokeshire for organised coasteering groups.

An easy path leads around the north side of the bay from the car park, past derelict quarrymen's cottages and along an old tramway used to transport stones down to the harbour, to reach

INFORMATION

Easy beach access at Abereiddy, with more challenging access to the water at other places along the route. The coast path involves a few steep climbs and goes close to the cliff edge at times. Toilets at Abereiddy and Porthgain.

DISTANCE: 7 miles
TIME: 4 hours walking, not including swims and pub stops
MAP: OS Explorer OL35 North Pembrokeshire
START & END POINT: Abereiddy beach (SM 798 313, SA62 6DT). Bring cash for the car park.
END POINT: At start (or use the bus from Trefin to return to the start)
PUBLIC TRANSPORT: The 404 Strumble Shuttle bus connects Abereiddy with St Davids and Fishguard, via Trefin, May to September. Out of season, use the Fflecsi, on-demand transport service (tfw.wales/fflecsi).
SWIMMING: Sandy beach at Abereiddy (SM 798 313), Blue Lagoon, closed off during seal pupping season (SM 795 315), Traeth Llyfn, (SM 802 321) and Aberdraw / Aberfelin near Trefin (SM 834 325)
PLACES OF INTEREST: Blue Lagoon flooded quarry and quarrymen's housing, Abereiddy watchtower, brickworks at Porthgain, mill at Trefin.
REFRESHMENTS: Porthgain's The Shed (SA62 5BN, 01348 831518) serving up seafood straight off the boat and the best fish and chips around. The Sloop Inn (SA62 5BN, 01348 831449) offers generous pub food portions and delicious crab sandwiches. Up the hill in Trefin village is Y Llong / The Ship (SA62 5AX, 01348 831798).

the lagoon. The lagoon is under the ownership of the National Trust. During the autumn in recent years they have closed it off to protect breeding seals who have chosen the shelter of the calm water and rocks at the back of the quarry as a suitable site for their vulnerable pups. Please respect the closure during this time, and check the website for updates as the dates of closure vary whilst the Trust monitors seal behaviour.

For the rest of the year, this is a wonderful place to swim, and a good option when other places are too rough. It is exceptionally deep, so much so that the Red Bull Cliff Diving championships were held here. Competitors launched themselves from a platform high up on the cliff tops above the lagoon. Look closely and you'll still see the structure that the platform was secured to. The water temperature here is generally a few degrees less than elsewhere, due to the depth. It is generally wonderfully clean, as on each tide the sea floods in and refreshes the water. Access is via a steep slope, then off the rocks at the back of the quarry – the level rises and falls with the tide. Many people are drawn here for the fun of jumping from the old quarry buildings on the far side of the quarry; there are different levels to jump from, depending on how brave you're feeling. The usual rules for jumping apply here and if you're not sure, consider joining one of the organised coasteering groups that run trips here most days. If you really want to enjoy this place at its best, come early in the morning before the crowds as it does get extremely crowded during sunny weekends and peak summer days.

2 After your swim here, retrace your steps along the tramway and climb up onto the clifftops. A small detour and a bit of a scramble takes you across to the watchtower, built following the last, failed, French Invasion (see Walk 13 for the full story). This is a wonderfully easy going walk along the clifftops towards Traeth Llyfn, one of the most beautiful beaches in Pembrokeshire, turquoise waters washing over gleaming sands, surrounded by the jagged cliffs so typical of this part of the coastline. Access to the beach is down a steep set of stairs. It is important to be aware of what the tide is doing as it is easy to become cut off here by the incoming tide.

3 The route continues along the clifftops and passes above two large open quarried levels, an odd lunar-type landscape which was formed by the extraction of stone during the 19th century. The stone was winched up, then transported by tram to the harbour at Porthgain for onward shipping. Our route continues on part of this old tramway, before descending to the harbour on a steep set of steps, and passing the old harbourmaster's office. On the right, enormous brick structures line the steep side of the harbour. These 'hoppers' stored crushed stone ready for shipping out across Wales and even to Dublin. Slate from the blue lagoon quarry was the first material to be exported here at any scale. It was mostly used for roofing during the house building boom of the 19th century, although it was inferior in quality, and couldn't compete with the vast amounts of high-quality slate produced in North Wales. The quarrying company turned to extracting stone for roads, and bricks made in the onsite brickworks using waste from the slate quarrying process.

Porthgain is still a working harbour, with crab and lobster the prime catches. It is an immensely popular tourism spot, visitors being drawn to the idyllic coastal charm and the iconic pub The Sloop Inn which dates back to the 18th century as a sailors' haunt. It is well worth stepping inside to see all the local maritime memorabilia hanging from the ceilings and adorning the walls.

The harbour itself, though technically swimmable at high tide, doesn't make for the best, or cleanest swim; it can be muddy and debris gets washed into and trapped in the harbour, plus there are plenty of hazards with the comings and goings of fishing vessels and kayaks. There are other, better options on this route. **4** Pass the lime kiln and continue up the coast path on the other side of the harbour, reaching one of the old bright white harbour beacons used to guide the ships in safely.

The clifftop path through fields towards Trefin offers great views over the spectacularly jagged and steep cliffs. It passes a modern stone circle before reaching a quiet coastal road leading down to a rocky cove known as Aberfelin, or Aberdraw below the village of Trefin. In calm conditions this is a wonderfully quiet spot for snorkelling, with caves to explore, though there can be rather a lot of seaweed and submerged rocks to contend with. At very high tide, some coasteering is possible near the top of the beach.

On entering the beach from the roadside, you can see the remains of an old mill on the left. This mill was used to grind wheat and corn for the villagers of this once-busy port over a period of five hundred years. Water from the nearby stream was diverted to power the wheel and turn the millstone, which can be seen in the interior of the building. A well-known poem in Welsh, 'Melin Trefin', was written about the mill's closure in the early 1900s by Archdruid William Williams, who went by the bardic name Crwys. The poem is poignant in that it describes the decline of this local tradition, such a key part of the community, and foretells the mill lying in ruins, melancholically, in the traditional Welsh cynghanedd poetry form.

Trefin is worth the walk up the hill if you'd like to visit the small museum here, or the excellent 16th century pub, Y Llong (The Ship). **5** Otherwise, our route circles back through pleasant farmland, with elevated views over the rolling fields over to the coast. **6** The route dips into the valley above Porthgain, then climbs again before finally descending back to Abereiddy, into the marshy valley formed as a channel for glacial meltwater after the last ice age.

DIRECTIONS

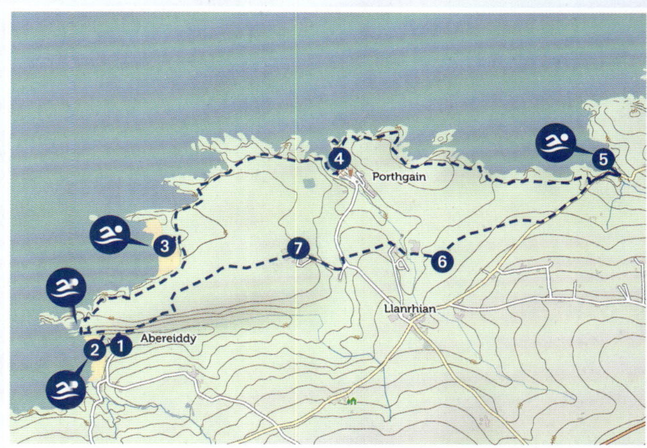

1 Begin at the beach, where you can have a first swim. Take the path at the rear of the car park which goes past the toilet buildings and turns back to pass the old quarry buildings. Continue on this path and cross a small footbridge to reach the Blue Lagoon for a second swim.
0.3 miles

2 Retrace your steps for a short distance along this path, then take the steep path going up to your left. Follow this onto the clifftops, around the edge of the fields keeping the sea close on your left. Follow the path as it bends round above Traeth Llyfn and begins to descend. Near the end of the slope find a set of steps on your left to access the beach for your third swim.
0.9 miles

3 Return to the top of the steps and turn left on the coast path which hugs the boundary fence on the right, keeping the sea on the left. When the path moves away from the fence, take the seaward path, following it down a set of steps to Porthgain harbour. Walk round the harbour with the water on your left, until you reach a lime kiln. You can explore the village if you wish and return here to continue.
1.1 miles

4 Follow the coast path uphill, again keeping close to the sea on the clifftops. Descend through a field past a modern stone circle. Then turn right, looking for a small gate where the field narrows, and go through it on to the road. Turn left and walk downhill on the lane, until you reach a small stream. Turn left and follow the path down to the beach. Trefin village is a short detour on the lane uphill.
1.8 miles

5 Return to the lane and turn right. Follow it back uphill, retracing your steps but continuing past the turning to the coast path, past the white house Awel For on the right, then through a kissing gate into a field on the right. Cross the field diagonally, cutting the corner and aiming for a gate in the hedgerow opposite. Go through the gateway and walk ahead, keeping the boundary on your left, until you reach a track. Follow the track until you reach a junction in paths at the farm.
1.1 miles

6 Turn left at the junction then, as the track curves left, look for the footpath into the field on the right. Walk to the right-hand corner of the field to enter the next field, then go directly ahead to a stile onto the road. Turn slightly left then take the right turning to go left along the driveway to Ynys Barri farm and holiday cottages. Follow the track as it curves right through the trees and continue until you reach the farm.
0.6 miles

7 Keep to the main track, with the holiday cottages to your left and a large barn to the right. Continue along the track through fields, ignoring the first footpath on the right and bearing left when you meet the second footpath coming in from the right. Continue on this footpath, which will bring you back to Abereiddy beach.
1 mile

Walk 12

ABERMAWR

An often-overlooked nook of the dramatic North Pembrokeshire coastline, here you'll find pebbly beaches with sands revealed at low tide, a stunning stretch of coast path seals to spot, peaceful woodland and a historic woollen mill.

Tucked away in a secluded wooded valley south of Fishguard, the spinning of a water wheel and rhythmic hum of weaving looms set the soundtrack for the beginning of an exceptionally pleasurable circular walk. The route begins and ends at Melin Tregwynt, an outpost of contemporary Welsh design with a long history. Run by the same family since 1912, the mill produces traditional Welsh woollen tapestries in hues inspired by the surroundings of the Pembrokeshire coast and countryside. It's an excellent spot to begin and end a walk; save time at the end to enjoy the café and visit the mill where you can see the weaving process in action. The bus stops outside the mill in season, and generally they are happy for you to park here while you walk if you're planning a visit afterwards, but it is always worth checking. Otherwise, there are a limited number of spaces for parking at the end of the little lane which runs down to Abermawr beach, from where you can start the walk.

From the mill, it's a beautiful walk down through woodland towards the coast, the anticipation of catching that first glimpse of the sea at the end of the path building as you get closer. Two traditional whitewashed stone cottages set back in the trees hark back to the days when sailors and smugglers would make their way down to the cove, the former for fishing, and the other for less illustrious purposes.

The twin bays of Abermawr and Aberbach (essentially translating as Large Rivermouth and Small Rivermouth) allow a reprieve from the jagged cliffs and inaccessible coves found on this part of the coastline. Even as recently as the 1980s smugglers

INFORMATION

A few steep climbs, wobbly rocks on the beach and muddy trails. Relatively remote swimming spots, which can be affected by strong currents and swell so a good level of competence and self-sufficiency is important. Seals breed on this part of the coastline so ensure no pups are present before swimming.

DISTANCE: 6½ miles
TIME: 4 hours walking, not including swims or visiting the mill.
MAP: OS Explorer OL35 North Pembrokeshire
START & END POINT: Melin Tregwynt (SM 894 348, SA62 5UX); car parking possible (see text)
PUBLIC TRANSPORT: The 404 Strumble Shuttle bus connects St Davids and Fishguard during summer months, with a stop at Melin Tregwynt. Out of season use the Fflecsi, on-demand transport service (tfw.wales/fflecsi).
SWIMMING: Aberbach (SM 884 351), Abermawr (SM 883 346), Penmorfa rocks (SM 873 348), Pwllstrodur bay (SM 866 338)
PLACES OF INTEREST: Melin Tregwynt, Cable Hut, site of Castell Coch, submerged forest at low tide in Abermawr after stormy seas.
REFRESHMENTS: The café at Melin Tregwynt (01348 891288, SA62 5UX) is excellent, serving up light bites, soups and delicious cakes packed with local ingredients. Further afield, the Farmers Arms in Mathry (01348 831284, SA62 5HB) is a popular traditional Welsh pub.

have had their sights set on Aberbach as a place to land their contraband. In 1986, during a stormy November morning, a re-purposed fishing trawler, the Minnou, attempted to offload its goods here. Five million pounds worth of cannabis was transferred into rubber dinghies before they capsized in the rough sea. Two men were swept into the sea and it all could have ended very badly for them had two undercover police officers not been camping on the beach overnight as part of 'Operation Bach'. They raised the alarm and the stricken smugglers were rescued and apprehended along with a number of others onshore. Despite this, the remaining crew on board the Minnou made their escape, landing at Dublin, where the port authorities unwittingly released them, before they were captured near the Scilly Isles. The drugs later washed up below the cliffs and were winched up as part of the recovery.

Today the scene that greets you when you arrive at the beach on a calm day belies the drama of the past. Mermaids feel more likely than drug gangs. Indeed, a local legend tells of a farmer who captured a mermaid from this very place, taking her back to his farm. That night a storm raged and the mermaid's mournful song awoke the farmer, who suddenly felt remorseful at having captured her, and released her back to the sea. On doing so, the storm immediately calmed. The stony beach and crystal water is instantly inviting but do take a minute to check for seal pups during late summer and autumn, and move on if they are present to avoid causing any disturbance. Otherwise, enjoy the peace and tranquillity of the turquoise sea and the views of the surrounding cliffs, drying off on the sun-warmed stones afterwards.

❷ A short walk across Pen Deudraeth (Head of Two Beaches) brings you to the larger of the two, Abermawr. On the lane above the beach, believe it or not, the unassuming hut now used as a holiday cottage was once at the very frontier of transatlantic communications. In 1866 an ambitious project to lay a telegraph communication under the Atlantic Ocean was completed: from Newfoundland the cable reached Ireland, then crossing land and into the sea again at Wexford, reemerging right here in Abermawr, enabling the first effective telegraph messages between North America and Britain. In 1922 the cables were damaged by a storm and communication technologies developed subsequently meant that the station was abandoned.

Brunel, too, had plans for developing the beach as a terminus for his South Wales Railway here at Abermawr, with onward passage by sea to Ireland, and began investigating the potential during the 1920s. Initial trackways were laid, but an alternative site was found and so the project never came to fruition. For that, the local seals are no doubt thankful.

If you're arriving by car and parking on the lane, you'll begin your walk here and descend to the

beach. Abermawr has a very steep bank of stones at the top, formed thanks to sea level rises at the end of the last ice age, combined with the continued action of the sea which pushes the rocks up the bank when the powerful waves often found here crash on the shore. This means that at high tide the sea becomes deep close to shore. There is often a strong undertow, so care must be taken of the powerful waves and currents. As the tide drops, an expanse of flat sand is exposed allowing for more easy-going swimming and splashing in the waves.

If you wanted, you could return on a path inland here through pretty woodland for a shorter alternative to the full route proposed here. ❸ But for those looking for yet more swimming and to enjoy this spectacular section of the coast path, continue across the beach, climbing steeply to gain the clifftops, with spectacular views back down the beach only getting better and better as you climb. Following the coast along, the path reaches a promontory, known as Penmorfa. Here an Iron Age Fort once stood. Today very little is discernible of the banks and ditches that would have provided defences for the fort, and a large part of the cliff has fallen away in recent years taking some of the fort remains with it, evidence of the rapid erosion occurring along this part of the coastline. On the gentler north-east facing slope of this promontory, a faint fishermen's path leading off the main coast path goes down to jagged, barnacle and lichen-encrusted rocks sloping into the sparkling waters cradled by the headland. Experienced and competent swimmers may like to explore here on a calm day; there is some fantastic snorkelling and you may find yourself joined by a curious seal or two, as we were on our visit. We nicknamed this spot 'the graveyard' as the rocks were scattered in fish and

bird bones. Some creature – perhaps an otter - clearly enjoys its lunch here on occasion.

Needless to say, this is a very exposed and remote spot and all caution should be exercised: choose your entrance and exit of the water carefully and spend some time judging the conditions. Should you have any doubts, wait for another day.

❹ The climb back up to the cliff path soon warms you up again. Rounding the headland the views open up to the south and west. It's a great wildlife-watching stretch, with seals, porpoises, choughs and peregrine falcons often sighted here. Drop down to the pretty horseshoe cove Pwllstrodur. Often sandy during the summer, there are submerged rocks to avoid here. It really feels like a hidden secret, where you can sunbathe, picnic or explore the rock pools.

(5, 6) Switching inland away from the coast, the route takes you through gentle countryside along a byway which feels ancient, returning to the coast for a short stretch before entering the wonderful National Trust woodlands which line the Abermawr valley (❼, ❽), and back to the mill on a quiet lane ❾.

DIRECTIONS

❶ From the bus stop outside the mill, head north along the lane which bends to the left. Turn right at the junction at the end, continuing up to a path next to a house on the left. Follow a grassy track through woodland and past the cottages to reach Aberbach beach for a first swim.
0.7 miles

❷ Walk south along the beach, climbing up onto the cliff path. Follow it round with the sea to your right and emerge onto a lane. Turn right at the lane and follow the path down to Abermawr beach, for the second swim.
0.5 miles

❸ Climb up the steep path at the far south side of the beach, following the coast path signs. Turn right at the top, then continue with the sea on the right. As the path begins to veer left (south-west) look for a faint path through the bracken. Follow this down a steep slope to the north-east to a set of lichen-encrusted rocks. Use your judgement to find the best entrance and exit to and from the water here depending on tide and conditions.
0.9 miles

❹ Return to the coast path, turn right and follow it until it descends to a small valley; turn right to reach the cove for the fourth swim spot.
1.1 miles

❺ Climb up from the cove and turn right, continuing to climb up on the coast path. Turn left at the gate to follow a public footpath inland. Walk through the field to a gate onto a lane on the far side. Turn left then left again on to a grassy byway before the house.
0.4 miles

❻ Carry straight ahead on this byway ignoring other turnings. When you reach a gate at the end of the byway, turn left to follow the track to the coast path and rejoin the route from earlier in the walk, walking in the opposite direction this time.
1.1 miles

❼ When you reach the path going back down to Abermawr beach, don't turn down, instead keep straight ahead and walk through the woods. Walk down the steps, then take the path to the left of the field. Turn left before the houses to a small footbridge over a stream.
0.5 miles

❽ Go over the footbridge and take the right-hand path. Go over another stream and through the gate to Broom Wood. Stay on the right-hand path through the woods. Continue ahead (right) at a junction of paths, emerging onto a lane.
0.3 miles

❾ Turn left on the lane and continue to a crossroads. Go straight over the crossroads and walk down the hill, turning left to return to the mill.
1.1 miles

Walk 13

DINAS ISLAND

A satisfying circular walk around a prominent headland, with panoramic clifftop views, two sandy coves for swimming, an old sailors' pub, tales of storms, invasions and a mysterious underwater world.

Dinas Island may be more of a headland than an island, separated as it is from the mainland by a tiny stream which dries up during prolonged warm spells. Nevertheless, sat outside the Old Sailor's Pub at Pwllgwaelod with a drink on a warm summer day as day trippers paddle and swim in the adjacent cove, and with only the tiniest of lanes in and out plus one small campsite, there is an unmistakeable island vibe to the place.

The island juts out into the sea from the coastline between Fishguard and Newport, and both coves are popular, becoming very busy during the summer. Begin in Pwllgwaelod, a sandy tidal cove, surrounded by Ordovician slate cliffs, which give the beach its dark sand. It becomes more spacious at low tide but can be a little cramped at high tide. Wonderfully sheltered, the sea in the cove is often calm, and offers a wonderful first swim for the day. Whether you want to simply go in for a dip, to splash around with the children, to snorkel around the rocks, or to go for a longer swim, you'll find Pwllgwaelod bay is great for all swimmers. A low tide swim to the neighbouring, cut-off, beach Pwll Cŵn will give you that desert island feeling when the main beach is busy. Swim out from the bay, keeping the cliffs on your left, the sandy bay is 300 metres away at low tide. It's wise to use a tow float here to be visible to boats which come in and out of Pwllgwaelod.

As you're swimming, keep an eye on the water below, for the mysterious fairy dwellings of legend. According to Sabine Baring-Gold, who wrote A Book of South Wales in 1905, the legend says that "under the sea by Dinas Point, in Pwll Gwaelod, lies a fairy

INFORMATION

A well-walked section of coastal path, steep in some places with steps and uneven parts. A very well made, flat track links the two coves directly. Toilets at Cwm yr Eglwys and Pwllgwaelod.

DISTANCE: 3½ miles
TIME: 2 hours, not including swims
MAP: OS Explorer OL35 North Pembrokeshire
START & END POINT: Pwllgwaelod car park (SN 006 398, SA42 0SE). Parking available here or alternatively at Cwm yr Eglwys.
PUBLIC TRANSPORT: The T5 Trawscymru bus service stops at Dinas Cross, 1 mile inland, connecting with the train and ferry in Fishguard or the train station in Haverfordwest.
SWIMMING: Pwllgwaelod beach (SN 004 399) and Cwm yr Eglwys beach (SN 015 401)
PLACES OF INTEREST: Remains of St Brynach's church (Cwm yr Eglwys) and Needle Rock seabird colony
REFRESHMENTS: Follow in the footsteps of Dylan Thomas at the idyllically located Sailors Safety, Pwllgwaelod, right on the route. Can get very busy in season (SA42 0SE, 01348 811486). The Ship Aground in Dinas Cross (SA42 0UY, 01348 811124) is a local pub with hearty pub food, beer garden, live music and a roaring fireplace. Otherwise head to Newport for a great range of options. Try Llys Meddyg (SA42 0SY,01239 820008), Blas at Fronlas(SA42 0PH, 01239 820065), or Tides Kitchen & Wine Bar (SA42 0PH, 01239 820777).

city inhabited by a mysterious people called the Bendith y Mamau (the Blessing of the Mothers). When the sea is calm, through the crystal waters can be seen the golden roofs and spires and marble palaces of the underwater folk. The vision lasts for from five to ten minutes at a time. One day a ship of a Dinas fisherman cast anchor in the Pwll, when up the chain came swarming one of these subaqueous people, who stepped on deck and said to the captain, "What is this that you are doing? Your anchor is in the roof of my house." The captain promised to disengage it and not cast anchor there again."

❷ Leaving Pwllgwaelod behind, the route will take you steeply uphill, climbing high on to the headland. There is a track that's very easy to follow, provided you keep the sea to your left at all times, which means you can't go far wrong. If you need to give your legs and lungs a break, take advantage of the ever-increasingly beautiful views, over the sea beyond Fishguard to its ferry port, and further west still to Carregwastad and Strumble Head.

The port at began operating for ferries to Rosslare in Ireland from 1906, with the same route still in operation today. In 1912, a flight across the Irish Sea set off from Fishguard, making pilot Denys Corbett Wilson the first person to successfully fly between Britain and Ireland.

The headland Carreg Wastad, just visible beyond Fishguard as you continue along the path, was the site for a more unwelcome international interaction, the last invasion of Britain. In 1797 French ships manned with more than 1,000 soldiers attempted to sail into Fishguard, having been blown past their intended port of Bristol by the strong coastal winds. They planned to build an army and invade England. A cannon was fired from the Fort at Fishguard, and the invasion retreated to Carreg Wastad. There was no welcome to be found there either: local woman Jemima Nicholas, a cobbler, also known as Jemima Fawr, Jemima the Great, organised large numbers of women to dress in their traditional costumes which resembled military dress of the era. They paraded along the clifftops imitating infantry, and the French Commander fell for the rouse. Believing they were outnumbered, the French surrendered. Jemima herself is said to have rounded up a dozen soldiers with her pitchfork and locked them in the local church. Jemima's legend lives on in various folk tales of the area. Several festivals and reenactments have honoured her. A memorial stone to Jemima and a tapestry of the last invasion can be found at Fishguard.

This peaceful, sleepy part of the coast, which only sees a couple of ferries depart and return each day, belies the comings and goings of the past. But as you climb high to the viewpoint, the drama of the sea panorama gives you the impression of being at the helm of a large ship, conjuring up a sense of maritime adventure. There is a trig point to mark the highest point, 142 metres above sea level, known as Pen y Fan, not to be confused with the mountain of the same name in the Bannau Brycheiniog National Park. It's a great place to have a break and take in the views; on a clear day you'll be able to see as far north as the Eryri mountains and the Llyn Peninsula, and perhaps even the Wicklow mountains of Ireland.

❸ The walk continues between the bracken-topped cliff path and fields; in spring there is a carpet of bluebells here. There is a choice between the lower path which takes you past Needle Rock – a seabird colony, noisy in early summer with guillemot and razorbill chicks. The lower path is precarious and those not fond of heights or with young children may wish to take the higher path; the paths meet up again later.

❹ The path descends through shrubbery and trees to the pretty cove of Cwm yr Eglwys. The eglwys (church) in question, St Brynach's, only has one wall remaining, after it was destroyed during the Great Storm of 1859. This storm famously sank the Royal Charter steam clipper off the coast of Ynys Mon, in North Wales. In all, 133 ships were sunk, and there was a death toll of more than 800 people. In response, the sea wall in front of the remains of the church was built to protect the village. On a warm summer's day, it is difficult to imagine such violent conditions. Cwm yr Eglwys is a very well sheltered spot, with a microclimate allowing subtropical plants to grow. It is a wonderful place to swim, and much like Pwllgwaelod, offers a range of swimming opportunities to suit all. Experienced swimmers can snorkel and swim or coasteer around the rocks to a pristine golden sand beach for more space when the main cove is crowded.

The annual Dinas Cross regatta is held here each year in August, with a variety of events organised by the local community over several days, including a long-distance swim from Aberfforest beach to the north, back to Cwm yr Eglwys. The regatta's other events include sailing, a raft race, fun run, yoga, crabbing and fishing, an open-air church service, quiz night and cream teas. The event celebrated its 125th anniversary in 2024.

❺ The route continues through the flat marshy valley which separates the headland from the mainland, formed by the action of glacial meltwater during the Quaternary glaciation. Yet another environment on this varied walk, the valley is wooded and offers shelter, habitat and freshwater for birds and insects not found elsewhere on the route. The well-made path returns to Pwllgwaelod near the pub, the 'Sailors Safety', a name which probably needs no explanation.

Dylan Thomas, the famous Welsh poet, once turned up at the pub in hope of a lobster dinner. According to John Malcom Brinnin, who was travelling with him in Wales at the time, and who wrote in his book Dylan Thomas in America: "There, just a few yards from the sea, was a somewhat ramshackle clapboard inn snugly sequestered between cliffs. We were the only patrons. The flustered proprietress, who obviously expected no one on this miserable evening, greeted us with notably more anxiety than pleasure. The promise of a lobster dinner which Dylan had used in goading us onwards was, it turned out, rather untenable."

DIRECTIONS

❶ From the car park, turn west to access the beach at Pwllgwaelod. Return to the lane near the car park, turn left, keeping the sea on your left. Before the lane bends away to the right towards a campsite, look for a gate on your left for the coastal path.
0.1 mile

❷ Go through the gate and follow the coast path keeping the sea on your left until you reach the trig point at Pen-y-Fan, Top of the Hill.
1.1 miles

❸ Follow the path along the fence line, you'll reach a broken wall and have the option to take a lower path, which takes you close to the seabird colony at Needle Rock, or to continue on the easier, higher path which sticks closer to the field boundary. The paths rejoin further down the hill.
0.9 miles

❹ Where the paths converge, continue through the trees and shrubbery until you emerge onto a lane in the village near a house. Follow the lane keeping close to the sea to reach the beach at Cwm yr Eglwys.
0.4 miles

❺ From the beach, walk up the lane next to the church remains, cross into the car park, through the caravan park at the back, then going through a gate onto a well-made track through the wooded valley. Continue until you emerge next to the Sailors Safety pub back in Pwllgwaelod.
0.7 miles

Walk 14

MOYLGROVE

A journey through wooded valleys to the wild reaches of the north Pembrokeshire coast, where cliffs fold and plunge into the ever-changing waters of Cardigan Bay. Three real adventure swims for calm days, one in a pretty cove, one in a natural 'swimming lane' and the other in the Witches' Cauldron collapsed sea cave.

INFORMATION

Good coast path, woodland tracks and lanes. The coast path goes very close to the edge at points so those with a fear of heights may find it challenging, and you may want to avoid it altogether in high wind. You need calm conditions for the swims; some rock scrambling is required to access the water at two locations and the cave swim is also tide-dependent. Toilets at Moylgrove.

DISTANCE: 5 miles, with 300 metres of ascent
TIME: 3 hours not including swims
MAP: OS Explorer OL35 North Pembrokeshire
START & END POINT: Moylgrove village car park (SN 118 446, SA43 3BW)
PUBLIC TRANSPORT: The Poppit zone Fflecsi service covers Moylgrove (tfw.wales/fflecsi) and links with the train at Fishguard.
SWIMMING: Ceibwr bay (SN 110 457), swimming off rocks (SN 107 458) and the Witches' Cauldron (SN 102 450)
PLACES OF INTEREST: Llech y Drybedd burial chamber
REFRESHMENTS: Nearest refreshments available in Cardigan or Newport where you're spoilt for choice. In Cardigan the Pizza Tipi has the best pizza around (SA43 1EZ, 01239 652259). Crwst bakery is a great modern café in the centre of town (SA43 1BU, 01239 611278). Yr Hen Printworks (SA43 1FA, 01239 612646) is an award-winning restaurant with small plates packed with premium local ingredients.

Moylgrove is an attractive little village tucked away in a wooded valley to the south-west of Cardigan. Although the English name is most commonly used, the Welsh name for the village, Trewyddel, means Irish Town. Given the long, historic Irish-Welsh connections on this part of the coast, the name comes as little surprise, but it does help to build a picture of what Moylgrove's past may have been like. The English name gives us further clues: 'Moylgrove' derives from 'Matilda's Grove . Matilda was married to the son of the Lord of Cemaes, and, on her marriage, gifted land at Moylgrove to nearby St Dogmael's Abbey.

The village is serene and full of characterful houses with attractive gardens. A wooded valley leads to the sea, and this is where our walk begins. It's a beautiful valley to walk through, a carpet of ramsons and bluebells lines the path in spring, with the song of newly-arrived chiffchaffs echoing above. In summer, ferns and a thick canopy lend a more exotic air to this little patch of would-be temperate rainforest. The stream is clearly mismatched to the size of the valley, which was carved not by the trickle of water which runs beside you, but rather a much larger scale activity associated with glaciation. Glacial deposits at the end of the valley further attest to this.

The magic of the woodland is over all too soon, but there's no time to mourn as you're greeted by a wonderful little cove, framed

by rugged cliffs, calling to you as you emerge from the trees. This is Ceibwr bay, a narrow rocky inlet, which offers wonderful swimming on a still day. On rough days the sea froths, boils and bounces its way through the cove, and is one of the last places you'd want to swim. During the great storm of 1859 merchant ship the Morning Star of Aberystwyth was wrecked here. Time your visit to calm conditions to get the most out of it. Snorkelling around the rocky cove edges offers much interest, and there are caves to explore. Out of the bay around to the west there is an almost perfect swimming lane formed by a mostly submerged rock running parallel to the coast. But this spot is better accessed from a bit further along the route, as only the very strongest swimmers would want to swim round to here, due to the potentially very strong currents at the mouth of the cove.

Ceibwr bay would once not have been quite as remote as it feels today. Moylgrove and Ceibwr bustled with activity back in the day. As with other villages along the coast, limestone and coal was brought into the bay on flat-bottomed boats. The remains of one of two lime-kilns can still be seen near here and a foundry was set up in the village to support the shipping trade. There were reportedly nine public houses in the area: two here at Ceibwr and the rest back in the village. ❷ To the west of the cove, there is a large flat grassy area, locally called Patsynglas, which was once used for village gatherings. You could imagine it would make an incredible camping spot, and it is from here that the next swimming spot is best accessed, by climbing down the rocks.

North of the bay, the rocks in the cliffsides show a wonderful display of folding, dating back to a great mountain building period known as the 'Caledonian Orogeny', some 390-490 million years ago. Much of this enormous mountain range has been weathered away; the folds and faults in the rocks here offer us a glimpse into this huge geological process. On that side of the bay the Pembrokeshire Coast Path makes its final miles to the end point at St Dogmaels. These are some of the toughest, and most dramatic miles of the entire trail, with steep climbs and precipitous plunges to the sea far below. ❸ Our route, heading south-west, is gentler, yet still clings closely to the cliff edge; those without a head for heights take heed! The views south-westward towards Newport are quite spectacular, with fingers of rock reaching out westwards, and blue waters washing over the jagged reefs, tantalising but out of reach. The path narrows and crosses an isthmus of sorts, a bridge, with sheer drops and water either side. To your left is Pwll y Wrach, or the Witches' Cauldron. It's an immense hole formed by the collapse of an enormous cave. The sea fills the hole at high tide, coming in through a passage through the

rock below the very place you are standing. This thought always makes me want to move a little faster to get to the other side of this natural 'bridge'. Not only that, but the emerald water is calling. It is worth saying at this point that there is a very strict ban on anyone entering the cave during seal pupping season, from late summer. This is prime seal territory and pups are known to have perished here recently because human disturbance caused their mothers to abandon them.

It is not immediately apparent how to get into the Witches' Cauldron, and you do have to time your visit carefully with the tide in order to swim through the cave. Things can go badly wrong in caves so to be safe, ideally go during the dropping tide, so that you have plenty of time to get in, enjoy being in there, and get back out again without having to worry about getting stranded in the cave. Do make sure that there is plenty of clearance before you swim through. Scramble down the rocks to the cove and get into the water, swimming towards the cave entrance in the rock to your right. If you can't see any entrance, it is probably because it is submerged with a high tide. There is a second cave entrance round the first point of rock on your right. There is also a tricky descent into the cave via the stream which drops into a hole, forming a waterfall below. This can be quite difficult to descend though, and because the cave swim-through is an experience not to be missed for the vibrant green waters within, opt for that way in instead. Once in the cave, there is a wonderful beach at the back, which would feel completely castaway if it were not for the coast path walkers looking down on you in amazement. It really is one of the most special wild swimming experiences in all of Wales, and a great adventure. Word however, is very much out about this place, so if you go at peak times during a summer weekend don't be surprised to be sharing it with lots of other adventurers.

❹ Turning back inland from the coast, we walk through a steep wooded valley known as Cwm Ffynon Alwm, named after a chalybeate spring once found here. Now lost to overgrowth, it was once used for bathing for its purported healing properties. It's another captivating and quiet woodland to wander through, alive with birdsong in spring and early summer. ❺ Passing a farm and walking up a track to join a lane, there is an option to take a short detour here to visit an impressive chambered tomb Llech y Drybedd, which translates roughly as 'Stone of Three Graves'. ❻ Standing in the corner of a field, it dates to the Neolithic period and is built similarly to the other Neolithic burial chambers in the area such as Pentre Ifan and Carreg Samson. ❼ An easy walk along the lane, which is generally quiet but may be busier in summer, brings us back to Moylgrove.

DIRECTIONS

1 From the village car park, cross the bridge over Nant Ceibwr, heading north, then walk steeply uphill on the lane. At a sharp bend in the lane, take a public footpath into the woods on your left. Continue through the woods on the path heading north-west, with the stream on your left, until you reach a house ahead with a bridge on your left. Turn left over the bridge then when the track joins the lane, turn right over the footbridge to reach the beach to swim in the cove.
0.9 miles

2 Return over the footbridge and turn right to follow a path above the western edge of the cove. As the path rounds the mound, you'll reach a flat open grassy area. Scramble down the rocks to reach the 'swimming lane'. Return to the grass and join up with the lane. Follow it uphill for a short distance then turn right on to the coast path.
0.4 miles

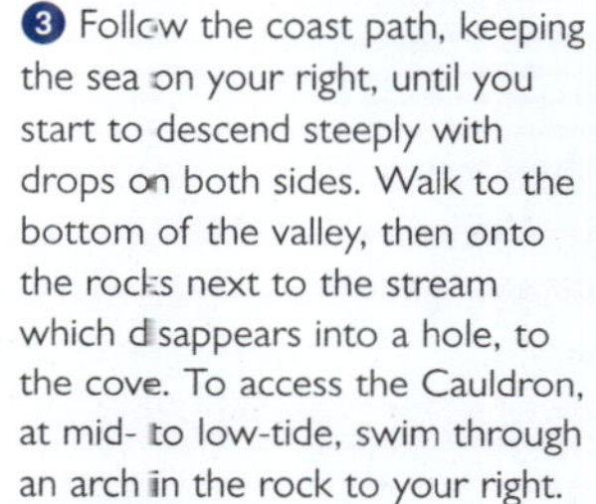

3 Follow the coast path, keeping the sea on your right, until you start to descend steeply with drops on both sides. Walk to the bottom of the valley, then onto the rocks next to the stream which disappears into a hole, to the cove. To access the Cauldron, at mid- to low-tide, swim through an arch in the rock to your right.
0.6 miles

4 Return to the path, heading south-west away from the Witches' Cauldron, and climb uphill. Take a footpath on your left heading inland, south-west then south into the woods. Follow the path at the top of the valley through the woods with a stream to your left. Then you emerge onto a farm track.
0.5 miles

5 Take the centre-right, not the furthest right, track, towards a farm. Turn right through the farm, then left up a track to join a lane.
0.5 miles

6 To visit the burial chamber, turn right along the lane then left onto a track. Follow the track to the end, bearing left at a bend. The burial chamber will shortly be to your right. Return to the lane.
1 mile

7 Turn right on the lane and follow it all the way back to the centre of Moylgrove.
1.2 miles

Walk 15

TEIFI GORGE AND CILGERRAN

Swim through the enchanting thickly forested Teifi gorge on the river's lower reaches, in one long swoosh or dipping in at different spots from the wooded riverbanks. Top it off with a visit to the medieval Cilgerran castle or the Welsh Wildlife Centre.

INFORMATION

Although short in distance, the walk through the gorge involves several steep climbs and descents on muddy and slippery slopes. The swim through the gorge is committing with few places to get out, and some shallower stony sections depending on river level. The Teifi can suffer pollution so check the Safer Seas & Rivers app.

DISTANCE: 4½ miles for the circular route, or swim 2 miles and walk 2½ miles

TIME: 3 hours excluding swims

MAP: OS Explorer 198 Cardigan and New Quay

START & END POINT: Cilgerran Lower Car Park (SN 198 430, SA43 2SS)

PUBLIC TRANSPORT: Bus 430 connects to Cardigan and Narberth, with onward trains at Clunderwen and Narberth

SWIMMING: Various points in the River Teifi (SN 197 430), (SN 189 453) or connect these with a longer swim

PLACES OF INTEREST: Cilgerran Castle, Welsh Wildlife Centre

REFRESHMENTS: Pick up a picnic and fresh coffee as well as lots of other local produce at Siop y Pentre, right on the route (SA43 2SG, 01239 621979). The Welsh Wildlife's Glasshouse Café has a gorgeous outlook and serves good light bites, warming soups and cakes (SA43 2TB, 01239 62121). For drinks the Rampin (Mason's Arms) is a great local pub in Cilgerran. Coracle Fish & Chips is a great takeaway option and can be found in Llechryd, a few miles away. Or head to Cardigan for a wide range of options as in Walk 14

The Teifi forms the boundary between Ceredigion and its neighbouring counties to the south, reaching the sea near Cardigan. With more than 40 tributaries this river was the very essence of mid-west Wales for centuries, if not millennia, shaping the way people lived, worked, dressed, ate, fought and died. From high up in the Cambrian Mountains the river flows through market towns, past ancient abbeys and castles, through wetlands and nature reserves, rushing in rapids and meandering calmly through meadows. At its lower reaches, the Teifi carves a deep gorge, steep-sided and densely vegetated, before its final flourish through the Teifi Marshes and St Dogmaels. During big tides the river can feel the effects as far up as Llechryd.

Cilgerran is a historic village, which grew around its mediaeval castle, sitting high on the southern banks of the gorge. Salmon fishing and subsistence agriculture provided its lifeblood and, later, slate quarrying. There are several options for a wonderful swim-walk here. This chapter describes the circular walk option with spots to dip in and out of the river to swim, but there is also the possibility of a long, committing swim all the way down the river, walking either the outward or the return leg. Our route begins at the lower car park next to the river.

Alternatively, you could park at the Welsh Wildlife Centre and follow either half of the circular walk upstream to swim back, or swim down and walk back up. If you do want to do this, a tow float is an essential piece of kit, both to assist if you need a rest

(though of course they are not life saving devices), and to store your clothes / car keys / wallet etc, as well as to be visible to other water users such as canoeists and paddleboarders who are regular users of this waterway. As you'd be in the river for a prolonged period, it would be a good idea to wear a warm wetsuit.

Swimming downstream is only suitable for strong, experienced swimmers, as there are only a few places where you can exit the water. It is worth bearing in mind the risks of fallen trees, shallow spots where rapids can occur or where you may have to walk over stones for a short distance, and other river swimming hazards. Needless to say, this should only be attempted in normal flow conditions. If you have any doubts, don't try it!

Whether you're swimming all the way or just walking and dipping, the first entry to the river is in the same spot, from the steps near the picnic area downstream from the car park. There is an obvious path down to the steps. You can swim upstream for a way here and float lazily back down if you'd like a taste of longer river swimming without committing to the whole gorge.

This area is a hive of activity and jollity with the annual coracle regatta and races during Cilgerran's Festive Week in August. Throughout the week the whole village gets involved in events from the horticultural show and youth theatre performances to treasure hunts, karaoke nights and BBQs.

Coracles have been used on the Teifi for fishing for hundreds of years, and the Teifi Coracle continues to be used today. A coracle is a boat made from willow and hazel, covered in calico or more recently fibreglass; originally hide or flannel would have been used to cover the boat making it river-worthy. Upriver in Cenarth you can visit the National Coracle Centre if you're interested in

learning more about the heritage of coracle fishing, and there are several informative display boards at the car park.

The Teifi was once replete in salmon and sewin (Welsh sea trout). Unfortunately, due to the river's drastically diminished health, including from a particularly nasty biodigester spill pollution incident in 2016 which devastated the river's ecosystem and fish populations, fishing is no longer a mainstay of the local residents. Despite being a river of such rich cultural and natural heritage, all is not well with the Teifi. Scandalously, pollution incidents are common here, and rarely is anyone held accountable.

Unfortunately, it is wise to give the water a miss on days during and following heavy rain even if the flow is reasonable, to avoid runoff from unsustainable agricultural practices and sewage overflows. Use the Safer Seas & Rivers app for water quality updates. You can help by reporting any signs of pollution you may see during your

time here. The rest of the time, take the usual precautions of covering any cuts and showering as soon as possible after swimming.

If you're walking and swimming along the way, the outward route takes you first uphill away from the river to the impressive castle high on the banks. Built originally, as so many Norman castles were, from earth and timber, the castle was attacked on several occasions by the Welsh, and changed hands numerous times until finally being claimed by Norman William Marshal, Earl of Pembroke, and rebuilt in stone. The castle is perhaps best known for its association with Princess Nest, said to have been the most beautiful woman in Wales. She married Gerald of Windsor, who built a castle, said to have been Cilgerran, to keep her safe from would-be Welsh suitors. Famously, Owain ap Cadwgan attacked the castle and abducted Nest. Gerald escaped via the rather unceremonious exit of the garderobe (toilet) chute!

Continue to the church and through the graveyard, where a fascinating stone holds an inscription in Ogham – an early Irish alphabet – and Latin dated to the 6th century. The route follows a quiet track past fields and the Fforest Farm lodge and accommodation, where you may find yourself in the midst of a wedding celebration! A good pathway meanders through woodland below a tall raised bank separating it from the Teifi, eventually emerging in the Wildlife Trust nature reserve. An important site for overwintering and migratory bird species, otter, water shrews, snakes, dragonflies, fish and deer, this is one of the best wetlands in Wales. Divert from the route here to spend some time birdwatching from the hides or learning more about the wildlife of the area in the visitor centre.

The next swim, or final exit point if swimming from upstream, is on the edges of the reserve, where the river widens and the gorge comes to an end. A stone and mud slope leads into and out of the river. There is a great large rock here for changing on. It's a peaceful spot which you may be sharing with geese, swans or ducks. Pay heed during the breeding season!

The return upstream follows a strenuous, challenging trail along the riverbank through the gorge. It can be muddy and slippery and has more ascent and descent than you may imagine and with the jungly atmosphere, particularly on a humid summer day, you could be forgiven for imagining you are on an Amazonian expedition!

There is another spot where you can get in and out about a third of the way along the return path, next to a canoe launch point. The path continues through the gorge, before climbing back up to the ridge top and then into the village, bringing you back out near the castle before descending once more to the river to finish.

DIRECTIONS

1 Begin at river level at the Lower Car Park. Here you can get into the water via the steps for a swim, or begin a longer swim downstream. If walking, take the path going downstream next to the river, then a left up a steep path which climbs up to the castle. Follow the castle walls around to the left, then emerging on to the lane, follow it to the castle entrance, with the option to go in and visit the castle.
0.3 miles

2 Turn left on the lane to reach the main road through the village. Shortly after a noticeboard on the right-hand side take a pathway into the church yard and walk through to a minor lane. Come out of the church and turn sharply left, continuing down a narrow lane. Take a footpath off to the right, cross a footbridge and walk between two houses. You'll reach another lane; turn left onto it, then look for a track on the right.
0.6 miles

3 Go down the track, turning right at the end, entering Fforest Farm / lodge / wedding venue. Take a path on the left into the woodland, which passes above the lodge buildings. Continue on this path through the woodland until you reach the wildlife reserve. At a fork in the path, take the upper path above the building, then the middle path. Follow it around the back of an old building where it can be quite overgrown, then turn right to reach the river. Turn left and follow the river as closely as possible. At the end of the trail turn right on a narrow muddy path to get down to the river for another swim. If swimming downstream, as the river widens at the end of the gorge, look for an opening on the left before the reed beds and, in summer, lily pads.
1.6 miles

4 To return along the gorge, return to the path, following it with the river on your left. Keep left, signposted for the gorge trail. Follow this trail past old quarries, it will climb and drop to river level again several times before finally climbing steeply up to the right, following a yellow arrow. Please note that the lower right of way marked on the OS map is not a good path and is more or less impassable, so it is best to stick to the waymarked route here. Continue to the top of the ridge where you'll have fields and farm buildings to the right, reaching a gate into a field.
1.5 miles

5 Go through the field keeping to the boundary on the left. You'll enter an area of woodland and bear right on a path into a field. Go through the field sticking to the line of trees to your left. Reach the lane, turning left then right behind a stone cottage. Follow the path over the footbridge and back up the other side on to the lane.
0.3 miles

6 Turn left on the lane, then take the left to the castle. Go around the castle then back down the path to the river. Turn right at the river and follow the path back to the car park.
0.6 miles

Walk 16

ABERPORTH AND MWNT

Enjoy the relaxed, holiday atmosphere at Aberporth, before following a quiet route through woodland and farmland with expansive views over the sweep of Cardigan Bay. Swim in remote coves and spot dolphins from the coast path.

INFORMATION

This walk follows woodland paths, fields, lanes and coast path. There are several steep climbs, with one very steep climb down to Traeth Gwyrddon, which may not be for everyone. Toilets at Mwnt beach, halfway.

DISTANCE: 11 miles, with 600 metres of ascent

TIME: 6 hours not including swims – take a whole day to really enjoy this route.

MAP: OS Explorer 198 Cardigan and New Quay

START & END POINT: Aberporth beach car park (SN 258 515, SA43 2DD)

PUBLIC TRANSPORT: Trawscymru bus T5 connects Aberporth to Aberystwyth, with connections to Fishguard and Haverfordwest, with options to connect with trains at either end, as well as at Goodwick.

SWIMMING: Mwnt Beach (SN 194 518), Traeth Gwyrddon (SN 234 520), Aberporth beach (SN 257 515)

PLACES OF INTEREST: Eglwys y Grog sailor's chapel, Foel y Mwnt hilltop fort

REFRESHMENTS: Caban Mwnt kiosk (01239 612408, SA43 1QH) is the perfect halfway lunchtime stop. In Aberporth, the Ship Inn (01239 810822, SA43 2DB) is a great pub. The Boy Ashore (SA43 2EP), also in Aberporth, has a beach shack vibe and serves delicious burgers, fresh fish, cocktails and local beers, right on the water's edge. There is also a good fish and chip shop in Aberporth, Caffi Sgadan (01239 811003, SA43 2DB).

Aberporth is a wonderfully laid-back community and beach destination, with a big focus on tourism. The clean, accessible and sheltered sandy beach here separates into two at high tide and joins together again at low tide. On a warm summer evening it feels as though the entire village heads to the beach to swim, paddleboard, stroll with their dogs or just enjoy chips for tea overlooking the sea while watching the changing colours of the sky.

Meaning 'Port at the Sea Mouth', Aberporth has been an established port since the early medieval period, though its history goes back to the 6th century and likely much earlier. The village experienced somewhat of a boom during the 16th century with ship building and herring fishing industries. You can still enjoy good fish here.

The route begins and ends at the beach, where you'll find all the facilities you need at the start and finish of your adventure. As you'll be returning here, you can decide whether you want to swim here first or at the end – or perhaps both. Low tide and high tide swims are equally enjoyable. At high tide some like to jump from the rocks separating the two parts of the beach. Always check the depth and that you're able to safely exit before doing this!

To swim here is to follow in the footsteps of generations of sea-lovers; sea bathing for leisure and health has been recorded here as far back as the mid 19th century.

The beach is lifeguarded during peak season so makes for a good safer swimming option. If you're thinking of swimming out or for a longer distance, a tow float and brightly coloured

swimming cap will make you more visible for other water users – it can get busy in the bay at times! Also be aware of the boat lane and avoid it.

Leaving the beach behind for now, our walk takes us first inland, away from the sea, through a small wooded valley, climbing up through the trees and fields to reach the village of Parcllyn. As you emerge from the valley the views over the curve of Cardigan Bay are spectacular. The T5 bus has a stop in the village so if you are travelling by bus, you could choose to get off and begin the walk here instead, saving the initial climb and retrace of steps later on. Parcllyn is a village which has grown to provide housing for the Ministry of Defence base which occupies the entire headland above Aberporth. There has been a military base here since the Second World War, which oversees military testing, including missiles and drone technology, in the Cardigan Bay area. A danger area covers much of the offshore water here, with target buoys that move regularly. If you were planning on doing any longer swims or swimming further out, you do need to consider this and do some research or contact the base for advice. The OS map, which provides an outline of the danger area, is a good place to start.

Moving away from the military base, our route passes towards wonderful beach at Mwnt through a small section of woodland and lush countryside and lanes packed with flower-lined hedgerows, with elevated views over the coastline. On a clear day, a panorama sweeping from Ynys Enlli at the tip of Pen Llŷn, along the peninsula's coastal hills, to the highest peak of Yr Wyddfa (Snowdon) and south to Cader Idris can be seen.

Descending towards the coast again, the distinctive conical shape of Foel y Mwnt appears ahead. A defended enclosure once sat atop this hill, dating back to the Iron Age. Below sits the impossibly romantic Eglwys y Grog, Church of the Cross. This name, dedicated to a cross rather than a saint, suggests an ancient origin to the church. The present building dates back to the 12th or 13th century, when it was used as a sailors' 'chapel of ease', meaning they could attend church without having to travel far. It is a beautiful, simple building, and worth a look inside if just to see the original font, sculpted from Preseli stone.

Legend tells of a Fleming invasion here in 1155. Henry II wanted to find a solution to overpopulation in Flanders, and also to regain England's control over west Wales, so sent Flemish soldiers to colonise Wales. A battle ensued and the Flemings suffered a bloody defeat. The battle was traditionally commemorated during January on 'Sul Coch y Mwnt' (Mwnt's Bloody Sunday), with games and a battle reenactment.

Moving on from gruesome history, a perfect horseshoe cove of golden sand appears below. Seals and dolphins make a regular appearance in the bay – in fact Mwnt is one of the best places to spot dolphins from the land in Wales. The sea can vary from calm and serene to huge waves dwarfing the bay and bouncing off the cliffs on each side, causing turbulent waters and sand banks and hollows. If you catch it on a day somewhere in between, it is great fun to play in the waves, and on the calmer end of the scale there is some coasteering to be enjoyed on the right-hand side of the bay below the hill.

You could spend plenty of time lingering here, enjoying lunch or an ice cream from the great little kiosk at the top of the beach, or climbing up to the top of the Foel which is ideal for dolphin spotting, and for the expansive views over to Cardigan Island and out to sea, which make the steep climb worthwhile. Sunsets here are spectacular, so should you be driving, you could begin and end here to catch the sunset at the end of your walk.

Continue along the route, following the coast path as it undulates eastwards, with several climbs down into and back out of small hanging valleys, all the while hugging the cliff edges which plunge into the wild seas below. Just as the path nears the headland occupied by the military base, a small and precarious-looking and grassy path snakes steeply down a slope towards the tiny cove of Traeth Gwyrddon (Verdant Beach). A good head for heights and surefootedness is needed here and walking poles would be an asset! For some this climb down will be beyond the comfort zone, and you may choose to give it a miss, but if you're happy to persist then you'll be rewarded with one of the most secluded swim spots around.

A stream carves a deep, narrow channel down to the beach and a set of steps has been cut into the rocks to ease access down onto the sand, though there is still some careful scrambling to be done; the rocks can be slick with seaweed. At high tide the beach disappears completely, when a swim is only really feasible off the rocks at the tiny mouth of the bay in the calmest conditions. At low tide there is a curve of sand, and caves to explore. If you're lucky you may be joined by a curious seal, or catch sight of a peregrine falcon as it swoops along the cliffsides above. This is really a very special spot but do take good care of yourself here as help isn't easily on hand.

There is an enjoyable return inland after making the steep climb back up from the beach, through the tree-lined valley and retracing your earlier steps into Parcllyn, before returning to Aberporth along the lane.

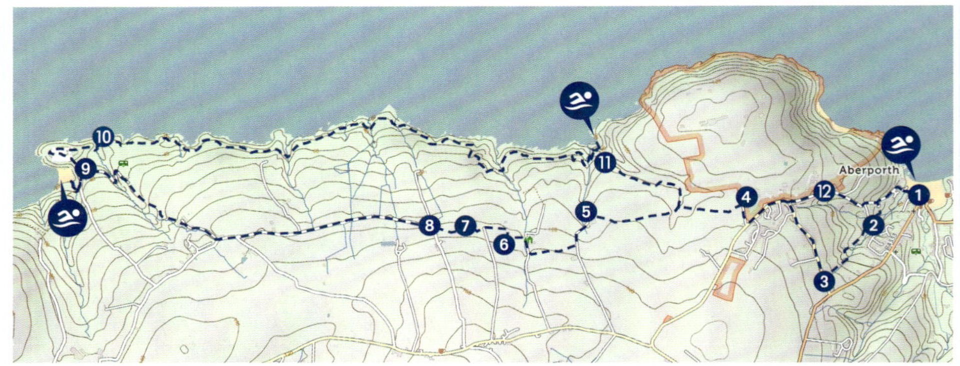

❶ From the car park, walk along Heol Pentraeth, heading along the eastern side of the beach then uphill on Rhiw y Rofft. Walk up the lane then turn left onto Cein Erw, signposted as a public footpath. Turn left down the driveway and go through a small gate ahead onto a path at the side of a house on your right, then next to a brook. Continue straight ahead, to the end of the houses on your left, and turn into the woods behind the final house.
0.4 miles

❷ Continue straight on this path, following the fence on your right. Be aware that the pathway here doesn't match the right of way shown on the OS map. Continue through the woods, and turn right before a barn, through a gate and uphill through a field to the gate at the top.
0.4 miles

❸ Go through the gate at the top of the field and turn right onto the lane. Follow the road through the village of Parcllyn coming out at the MOD base. Turn left and follow the road to the corner of the MOD fence, turning down the track, to a gate on the left before the barrier.
0.7 miles

❹ Walk diagonally across the fields to a gate into the trees, following the white topped marker posts. At a fork in the path turn left, ignoring the coast path signs. Continue through woods to a gate into a field. Turn right through gate and follow the hedge on the right to the bottom right-hand corner, where it joins a track. Take a left along the track to a farm.
0.7 miles

❺ Go through the gate, through the centre of the farmyard then follow the lane as it bends left then right, gently uphill. Look for a gate into a field on your right marked by a public footpath signpost. Follow the path through the fields keeping to the hedge line, then join a track, turning right then left on the track past the house.
0.6 miles

❻ Look for an easily-missed path into trees on your left to another field. Go straight across, following the direction of the telegraph poles towards the derelict house and barns ahead. Go through the gate then take a left through another gate. Stay in this field, keeping to the boundary on the right. The right of way on the OS map is shown on the other side of the fence but the path is not there so stick to the field you're in, reaching the far right corner where there is a sometimes-overgrown path on the right to a gate.
0.3 miles

❼ In the next field, keep to the left of the fence on your right, and at the far end go through two gates through the hedge in the corner on to a lane.
0.1 miles

❽ Continue straight ahead on the lane walking west. Turn right at a bend in the road next to a house, over a cattle grid. Continue downhill on the track, past a farmhouse and caravans. Turn left as you reach a crumbly cottage, and go through the gate between the cottage and barns. Pass more caravans and continue on the lane until you reach Mwnt beach car park.

2 miles

❾ Turn left and then right onto a pathway, past the toilets and kiosk then left again down the steps to reach the beach for a swim. Return back up the steps then take the optional steep climb up to the top of the hill above the church. From the top, follow a steep path down the other side to reach a narrow path on the other side. Turn right and continue following the path until you reach the coast path at narrow dip with a stream. Or, if you want to give the hill a miss, continue on the coast path which passes the church heading east.

0.7 miles

❿ Continue following the coast path with the sea on your left until reaching a footbridge just before the path swings inland in front of the MOD-occupied headland. If you want to access the cove below for a third swim, take the steep grassy track on your left through the bracken. If you enter the woods you've gone too far and missed it. After your swim return to the coast path.

3 miles

⓫ Follow the coast path signs into the woods, turning away from the coast. Continue straight on over the track then take a left out of the woods. Here you'll retrace your earlier steps through two gates and through the fields back out to Parcllyn at the MOD base.

1 mile

⓬ Keep ahead on the lane and then take the left-hand lane which returns you to Aberporth beach.

0.9 miles

Walk 17

LLANGRANNOG AND PENBRYN

A circular walk packed with history and legend, along a coastline of breathtaking beauty, to a wide sandy beach, a secret sheltered cove and a characterful seaside village, returning through tranquil countryside.

Penbryn is found down a narrow winding lane a mile or so from the main coastal road. The route first crosses the Hoffnant, a river just two miles in length from source to sea. It then continues through a wooded valley known locally as Cwm Lladron, Thieves Valley, seemingly having been a route inland for those involved in smuggling and illicit raiding of shipwrecks in centuries past. The residents of the valley once had a dubious reputation for these activities, much to the consternation of the clergy of the time. Local legend tells of one particular occasion when locals drank so much French wine plundered from a wreck that several of them dropped dead!

Penbryn was associated with legend long before the smugglers and wreck-raiders. The Battle of Llongborth is thought by some to have occurred in this very place, during which a great leader of Welsh tradition, Geraint, was killed. A few miles inland is a place named Beddgeraint, Geraint's Grave. His story was made famous by Tennyson in the poem 'The Marriage of Geraint'. Geraint appears earlier in the story of Culhwch ac Olwen in the Mabinogion, as well as the Welsh poem 'Geraint, Son of Erbin' in the 13th-century Black Book of Carmarthen. References to Geraint associate him with King Arthur, and date him to this area in the 6th century.

The days of shipwrecks and smuggling have long passed, and there are few battles nowadays, except perhaps for the last piece of cake in the Plwmp Tart café, and it's all peaceful and pretty. While most visitors will head straight down the lane from the car park to Penbryn beach, this alternative route offers a welcome

INFORMATION

Mixed terrain: expect some mud, sandy paths, rocks and grassy clifftops. Steep section of rock scrambling to access the middle beach, and walking down steep slopes. You may encounter some cows on the return route.

DISTANCE: 5 miles
TIME: 3 hours not including swims or stops
MAP: OS Explorer 198 Cardigan and New Quay
START AND END POINT: Penbryn National Trust Car Park (SN 296 521, SA44 6QL)
PUBLIC TRANSPORT: The T5 bus service which travels between Aberystwyth and Haverfordwest stops at Sarnau on the main A487 road 2 miles inland from the route. For many years the Cardi Bach coastal bus service (no 552) has served Llangrannog and Penbryn during the summer. At the time of writing the future of this service was uncertain, so please check before you travel.
SWIMMING: Penbryn beach (SN 293 525), Traeth Bach (SN 300 535), Llangrannog beach (SN 310 542)
PLACES OF INTEREST: Castell Bach and Pendinaslochdyn Iron Age forts, statue of St Carannog, RNLI barometer just outside village shop Siop Glynafon
REFRESHMENTS: In Llangrannog. The Pentre Arms (SA44 6SP, 01239 654345) offers pub food in generous portions. Tafell a Tân (SA44 6SN, 01239 654675) has the most delicious wood-fired pizzas around.

pocket of shade and lush vegetation to begin, with enormous ferns forming the undergrowth and a canopy formed by salt-tolerant sycamores.

Emerging out of the woods, you'll catch glimpses of the blue sea and sky framed by the trees. The beach is a large swathe of sand backed by cliffs, and there are caves to explore at the far north end. The sea is wonderfully clear and water quality here has consistently been rated excellent. Swimming is possible at all stages of the tide, and the beach is gently sloping, often with gentle waves, making it popular with families. Even though, as with most sandy beaches in Ceredigion, it can be extremely busy during summer weekends and holidays, the expanse is enough for the throng at the car park to disperse and to be able to find a quiet spot to swim and sunbathe or picnic.

After a first swim here, join the Wales Coast Path which returns on the lane almost all the way to the car park and café, and then climbs steeply along a flower-lined track to the clifftop fields, with phenomenal views all along the coastline, Penbryn beach now far below you.

Having reached a high point, the trail rounds a corner and you're greeted with the jaw-dropping beauty of a perfect arc of golden sand and turquoise water below. Although not named on the map, the beach is known locally as Traeth Bach or Morfa Cove, and is surely, if not the most appealing 'secret' beach in the whole of Wales, then certainly along the Ceredigion coast. It appears to be impossible to reach, and admittedly is not the easiest beach to access, but that is part of the magic.

Descend all the way to the bottom of the valley where a small stream cuts through, and follow a narrow path out towards the sea. Great care must be taken when descending to the beach; it involves some tricky scrambling down that will be enjoyable for adventurous folk, but is not for the faint-hearted. It can however, be managed with care by most and the rewards of squeaky golden sand and crystal sheltered waters are well worth it. There is a lot of exploring that can be done here too; you could scramble over the rocks to Carreg y Ty Island where a cave runs the entire way through the island. Seals may be in residence in late summer so do avoid disturbing them if this is the case. Beware of the tide so as to avoid getting cut off. The bed of flat rocks just off the island holds the grim tragedy of a group of young women who went out to sunbathe but all perished when they attempted to swim back having been cut off from the tide – you have been warned! Otherwise, it is a truly unforgettable place for snorkelling, coasteering, swimming and rock-pooling.

If you can tear yourself away from this most beautiful slice of Welsh paradise, make your way back up the rocks and rejoin the coast path, heading north-west. Towards the top of the steep hill the path passes through an Iron Age hilltop enclosure, Castell Bach, with visible banks and ditches. Alone this is impressive, but as you continue on the coast path Pendinaslochdyn fort, dated to a similar time, is situated on the prominent flat-topped headland in front of you on the opposite side of the bay.

Considered one of the best-preserved forts on this part of the coastline, defences can be seen, and excavations showed remains of a roundhouse. The same site is now home to a Ministry of Defence missile tracking station, which you can see on the hilltop from our route.

Descending to Llangrannog, you'll pass the statue of St Carannog, recognised as the founder of the village. Carannog was the grandson of Ceredig, the great leader from which the county of Ceredigion takes its name. Carannog rejected his opportunity to become leader of South Wales and instead went to live the life of a hermit in a cave at what is now Llangrannog. The village is separated into two: the area right next to the beach, and the earlier part near the church. This is said to have originally been founded in the 6th century near to the cave where Carannog lived. He dedicated himself to the early Christian religion and travelled to Ireland, Cornwall and Somerset. Legend has it that as he was crossing the sea near the Bristol Channel, the altar with which he travelled fell overboard, and Carannog asked for King Arthur's help to retrieve it. In return, Arthur requested his help in dealing with a troublesome dragon that was causing a nuisance. Carannog duly tamed the dragon, which thereafter caused no further problems.

Llangrannog later became a busy port with herring fishing. It is said that huge shoals could be easily found just offshore, making easy pickings for the locals, who were somewhat jack-of-all-trades, combining fishing and farming to make a living. Salt was imported, and herrings were salted and, along with butter, exported to Ireland and elsewhere along the coast. As in any navigable cove along this coast, boat building was also carried out in the village.

The famous English composer Edward Elgar visited Llangrannog in 1901. He later told of how some of his compositions were inspired by singing he heard while wandering the beach and village. And he was not the only high profile creative to visit the village. A local tale tells of a visit by Dylan Thomas to the Pentre Arms on the sea front, also the haunt of 20th-century Welsh poets T Llew Jones and Dic Jones. Thomas was reportedly expelled from the pub having been caught helping himself to drinks behind the bar.

The beach can feel busy at low tide, but once you're in the water, in calm conditions you can swim along the coast to find more secluded patches of sand. With the tide out, there is much more space, and with caves to explore and mini coves to wade to, the beach is great for exploring, with water great for snorkelling. There are plenty of places to refuel and use the facilities before continuing on the last leg of the walk. Before you leave the village, keep your eye out for a barometer situated in a glass cabinet next to the village shop. The barometer was given to the village in 1911 by the RNLI to help seafarers forecast the weather.

The route returns inland to Penbryn, through verdant countryside, farmland, and lanes and tracks lined with flower-packed hedgerows.

DIRECTIONS

❶ Walk through the car park towards the trees and find the footpath that descends to a stream. Follow the footpath back up the other side and then turn right. When the path splits, take the lower-right path which stays closer to the stream through the valley. Continue until you reach a footbridge and Penbryn beach.
0.4 miles

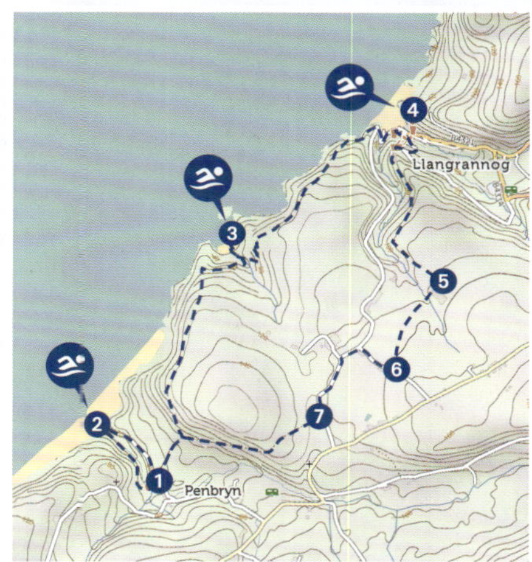

❷ From the beach, walk inland along the lane. Just before you reach the café and car park, take a left turning through a gate onto a track. Follow the track uphill, and go into the field ahead, keeping to the left-hand side. Exit the field, head downhill, then turn right. Follow the path around until you reach a small stream in a valley. Turn left at the stream and walk down a narrow path towards the sea. Scramble down over the rocks with care to reach the beach.
1.3 miles

❸ Return to the path and turn left, uphill. Follow the path with the sea on your left until you reach St Carannog's statue overlooking Llangrannog beach. Follow the lane nearest the sea, downhill into the village and to the beach.
1 mile

❹ Take the lane which heads inland behind the shops, cafés and toilets. Follow it uphill as it curves to the right then left, and passes houses becoming a grassy track through trees. Continue on this track as it skirts the valley until you reach the farm at Eisteddfa.
0.8 miles

❺ Turn right and then take the footpath into the field behind the barn. Cross a small stream, which may be muddy and overgrown. Enter a field on the other side, and follow the boundary on the right, then ahead on a track to reach a lane.
0.4 miles

❻ Turn right on the lane, then follow it left and left again. Look for a path to your right, signposted between hedgerows.
0.4 miles

❼ Follow the track ignoring two paths on the left. The track will meet with the coast path where you can turn left and retrace your earlier steps to the café and car park.
0.7 miles

Walk 18

CWMTYDU

Swimming options abound on this varied, short yet moderately challenging route. Remote rugged coves where renowned smugglers once landed their contraband, freshwater pools and cascades, quiet woodland and wild coastal path all await.

INFORMATION

Mixed terrain: fields, stiles, some mud, and can be overgrown in one or two places at the end of summer. Rocks and grassy clifftops. Some walking up and down steep slopes and steps.

DISTANCE: 4½ miles
TIME: 2 hours not including swims
MAP: OS Explorer 198 Cardigan and New Quay
START & END POINT: Cwmtydu village car park (SN 355 575, SA44 6LQ)
PUBLIC TRANSPORT: For many years the Cardi Bach coastal bus service (552) served Cwmtydu during the summer, five days per week. At the time of writing the future of this service is uncertain, so please check before you travel.
SWIMMING: Sea swims at rocky coves in Cwmtydu (SN 356 575), Traeth Soden (SN 363 583) and below Castell Bach (SN 359 579). Pool in river (SN 356 569), waterfall showers and dips at Nanternis (SN 366 579).
PLACES OF INTEREST: Castell Bach Iron Age promontory fort, waterfalls at Nanternis
REFRESHMENTS: The nearest option for food and drink is Caffi'r Hen Ysgol at Cross Inn (SA44 6NG, 01545 578322) with breakfasts, lunches, cakes, etc. and also pizza, craft beer and music nights. Slightly further afield is the Moody Cow farm shop and Bistro at Bargoed Farm, before you reach Llwyncelyn (SA46 0HL, 01545 580947) worth the trip for a delicious range of fare based on local produce.

Cwmtydu is tucked away at the bottom of a steep-sided woodland valley, just a few miles from the main coast road. Yet, on arrival you're transported to a world away, one of coves and caves, smugglers, seals and stars; this is a Dark Sky Discovery site!

The route begins at the cove of Cwmtydu itself, a horseshoe-shaped slope of sand and stones surrounded by colourful cliffs and deep caves, lapped by sparkling turquoise water, or thrashed by a swirling grey frothy mass, depending on conditions. At the end of summer into autumn this is an important seal nursery: females give birth to their pups in the caves surrounding the cove, moving them out onto the main beach if a big tide comes in.

Seals are not the only ones to have made use of the cove's secluded position over the years. Fabled smuggler Siôn Cwilt, a character made famous through Welsh-language author T. Llew Jones' children's story 'Lawr ar Lan y Môr', was said to have smuggled vast quantities of contraband through the cove. He got away with it for years by employing the locals to help unload the boats, buying their silence, and supposedly paying the local sheriff off with unlimited brandy!

The experience of swimming here depends greatly on sea conditions, with sand coming and going, scraped away by big seas and deposited during calmer times. In still weather the cove is beautiful for a gentle swim or snorkelling around the rocks. In rougher conditions the experience will depend on how much sand there is on the beach at that time – use your judgement and go carefully. Please refrain from swimming here from late August to December to avoid

causing a disturbance during seal pupping season. Even if you can't see any pups, they may be tucked away in the caves with their mothers keeping watch, easily scared off by human presence, especially in the water. A high tide swim is great as the sloping beach means it becomes deep quickly, though the beach does get swallowed up and becomes more crowded when the sea is in, especially during summer weekends. Beware of an undertow at high tide.

Leaving the cove behind, turn inland and walk up the slopes of the valley, with views of verdant countryside stretching ahead. Leaving the wooded track behind, descend a short way back to the valley floor on a winding lane past pretty cottages and fields of horses. If you want to skip the climb to get here you can simply follow the lane away from the beach instead; the chosen route is prettier though. You'll arrive at a bridge over the stream which runs through the bottom of the valley. ❷ Scramble down on the downstream side of the bridge – you may have to negotiate a bramble or two – and you'll reach a stunning little pool perfect for a cooling freshwater dip. It is said that salmon and sewin (sea trout) can be found here. Avoid scuffing the bottom of the pool, which is usually deep enough to avoid doing so in any case

Continue on the lane for a short distance, passing the entrance for Felin Huw – a post-medieval corn mill, before following a track uphill beneath towering, twisted oak trees. Climbing high up, views open up over the valley behind, thick with trees. The route continues through fields and attractive countryside, where the rights of way are well signposted around the side of a large house and small campsite, joining small winding lanes for a short while past more farm buildings.

You'll drop down again to walk along a track and through the meadows of another secluded valley at Nanternis. Reaching woodland once again there is a set of enchanting waterfalls along one of the streams that runs through the valley. ❸ The pools are not deep; the one at the very bottom is perhaps the best option for a dip, though it does take a little scrambling to reach. Tread carefully to respect the mosses and ferns in this micro-rainforest haven.

Leaving the woodland behind, the path clings high to the side of a valley, Cwm Silio, trees giving way to gorse and bracken. This landscape is managed by the National Trust, specifically to help conserve pearl-bordered fritillary butterflies – named for the 'pearls' that can be seen dotting the underside of the lower wing. Look out for a striking bright orange with black dots and lines on the wings. Management of the land has encouraged flowers such as dog violets to thrive, a key food source for the caterpillars, which are clinging on here in one of the few sites that they can be found in Wales.

The view of the sea opens out ahead of you as you walk towards the coast, offering tantalising glimpses of turquoise water. The same stream which cascades through the woodland behind you reaches its conclusion here at the beach, and fresh water often pools behind the storm-piled rocks at the top of the beach.

Traeth Soden, also known as Cwm Silio beach, has a true sense of remoteness, with no road access, buildings or facilities nearby. ❹ It feels like a wonderfully wild place to swim. The stony, sloping beach gives way to sand at low tide, and there are a few small caves to explore. Much like at Cwmtydu, conditions can vary wildly, and the slope can create difficult entry and exit to the water in rough conditions at high tide. Seals also use this beach on occasion for pupping, so keep an eye out and if any seals are present during the breeding season don't swim.

After swimming and perhaps a picnic there is a steep climb up to the clifftop, joining the coast path. The views here are spectacular. Continuing along the path you'll reach a large open grassy area with visible ditches and banks; these are the remains of Castell Bach, an Iron Age promontory fort. It isn't known whether the grassy stacks just offshore here were part of the hill fort originally or not; there is a possibility these were attached to the land at the time of construction and occupation and erosion has cut them off since.

You can descend a narrow and steep path to reach the beach below, suitable for swimming in very calm conditions only, as it is very rocky here. **5** Adventurous and experienced swimmers could swim around the island, taking care of currents. The beach is surrounded by wild flowers growing in the shingle and sandy cliffs: thistle, chamomile, knapweed and thrift all grow in abundance, attracting a whole host of insects. The stacks display incredible folded rock beds which will delight geology enthusiasts.

Returning back to the coast path, which clings precipitously in places to the cliff edges, where heather and gorse flourish in late summer, kestrels hover overhead. You may even encounter an adder, as we have, basking on the warmth of the stony coast path, or underneath some bracken. Don't fear – they're shy creatures and will usually slither away.

Keep an eye out in the water here for dolphins; it is possible to see them regularly from land along this stretch of coast path. As you descend to Cwmtydu, ahead in the distance you can spot Foel Mwnt and Cardigan Island.

DIRECTIONS

1 From the seafront, turn and follow the lane inland past the row of houses. Cross the bridge next to the toilet block. Follow the path as it bears left inland and up through woodland on the Wales Coast Path.
0.5 miles

2 When you reach the gate at the top of the path, turn left, leaving the Wales Coast Path, past some cottages, until you reach a bridge. Climb carefully down below the bridge on the downstream side to find a pool.
0.3 miles

3 Return to the lane, cross over the bridge then turn right along another lane. On the curve in the road near the entrance for Felin Huw, take the track heading up into the woodland on your left. Follow it all the way up to a gate, and take the steps to a sometimes-overgrown path, coming out on to the top, turning left through a gate into a field. Follow the fence line along the fields, behind a barn and house, through another gate and join a lane.
0.8 miles

4 Turn right, then left at a junction where there is a mounting block in the hedge. Continue on the lane which bears right at a farmhouse.
0.3 miles

5 Go past the farmhouse, take the lower track down through some woods, reaching a bridge and cluster of houses at the bottom. Turn left then take a right into the woods, merging on to a track. Keep going all the way down through the woods, reaching an open area.
0.8 miles

6 Bear right then follow the track to a footbridge. Turn left without crossing the footbridge, coming to a small stream. Turn right to follow the stream along a muddy track, reaching a series of cascades. Follow the cascades all the way to the bottom to find the deepest pool.
0.3 miles

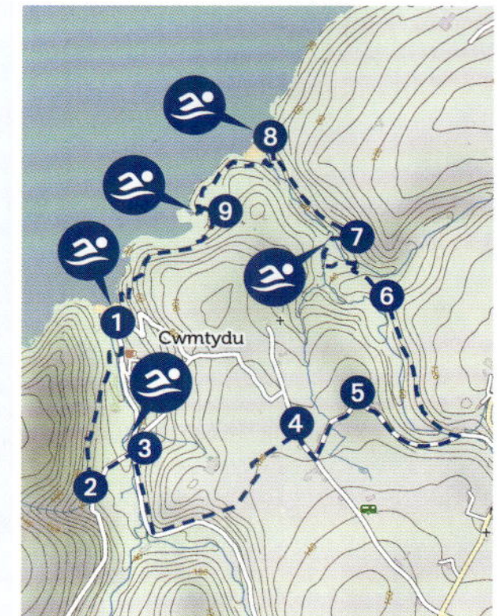

7 Return to the path and turn left to climb uphill, joining a main path through the valley, heading north west to the sea. Cross the bridge and go through the gate to reach the beach.
0.4 miles

8 With your back to the sea, climb up the steep steps on your right, joining the Wales Coast Path. Follow the path to a large open grassy area. If you follow the cliff edge round with the sea on your right you'll see a narrow and steep stony path leading down to the hidden beach below.
0.3 miles

9 Return to the coast path, climb up the hill and then follow it with the sea on your right all the way back to the cove at Cwmtydu.
0.6 miles

Walk 19

ABERYSTWYTH TO BORTH TRAIN WALK

Uncover the tale of a lost land, marvel at a five-thousand-year-old submerged forest, learn about Wales' first university town, and swim in the soothing waters of Cardigan Bay with no less than three lifeguarded beaches to choose from, plus two wilder swims. A short hop on the train completes the loop of this superlative coastal walk.

There are a couple of ways you could choose to do this walk. The train connection between Borth and Aberystwyth offers a wonderful chance to explore a long section of the Ceredigion (Cardiganshire) coastline, and the good connections make this a great public transport-friendly walk. If beginning in Borth, first take the train to Aberystwyth then start the walk from there or, if setting off from Aberystwyth, walk first and make the return journey by train later. I always prefer to start with the train in case of any delays later.

No guide book about swimming in west Wales worth its salt could neglect to include Aberystwyth, a favourite Victorian sea bathing resort. People once travelled here from miles away to take to the water for health and relaxation. Aberystwyth, or 'Aber' as it is locally and affectionately known, is at the mouth of the Rheidol and Ystwyth rivers. It is the Ystwyth river which gives its name to the town. Flint tools have been found in the area where the harbour is now, from a settlement of hunter-gatherers some seven to nine thousand years ago. The land would have looked vastly different then to how it appears today, as we will discover later in the walk.

The area was also occupied during the Neolithic period and later; the largest Iron Age hillfort in Ceredigion was built on the prominent hill now known as Pen Dinas, to the south of the town.

The Normans built their first earth and timber castle at Aberystwyth in 1110, but years of battling, seizing, destroying, rebuilding

INFORMATION

This route involves rollercoaster-like coast path with some steep climbs and descents. The path can be rocky and muddy in places.

DISTANCE: 7 miles, with 365 metres of ascent
TIME: 4 hours not including the train, swims or stops
MAP: OS Explorer 213 Aberystwyth & Cwm Rheidol
START & END POINT: Borth Train Station – or take the train to Aberystwyth to begin the walk from there.
PUBLIC TRANSPORT: Trains and buses widely available to Aberystwyth. The train journey between Borth and Aberystwyth takes about 15 minutes, runs hourly, and costs around £2 per person.
SWIMMING: Aberystwyth South Beach (SN 579 814), Aberystwth North Beach (SN 583 820) – both lifeguarded during the summer, Clarach Bay (SN 587 837), Wallog (SN 590 859), a rocky cove swim (SN 600 884) and Morfa Borth, also lifeguarded during the summer at (SN 607 890)
PLACES OF INTEREST: Aberystwyth Castle, Old College, Aberystwyth pier, National Library of Wales, Aberystwyth's funicular railway, Camera Obscura, Sarn Gyfelyn, Borth submerged forest
REFRESHMENTS: In Aberystwyth, Baravin (SY23 2AP, 01970 611189) on the sea front is a favourite. In Borth, great pub food is on offer with fresh seafood and a deck overlooking the beach at the Victoria Inn (SY24 5HZ, 01970 871417).

and recapturing the castles here ensued. The current castle was constructed by Edward I. It is on the South Beach, overlooked by the castle, Pen Dinas and the harbour wall that there is the chance to have a first swim before setting off properly. The South Beach is a steep, pebbly and sandy beach below a row of brightly coloured houses and a promenade, and is quieter than the main beach. It's a sunny, sheltered spot and the temptation is to linger here, sunbathing on the warm pebbles and swimming, until you remember that this is the only the first of six places you can swim today.

Moving on, pass the castle and the Old College, a striking historic building which housed Wales' first University from the 19th century. ❷ Today it is still part of the university, but undergoing redevelopment which is not due to be completed for some time. You'll then pass the pier, dating back to 1865, when it was opened to coincide with the Great Western Railway being extended from Machynlleth to Aberystwyth. This was Wales' first pleasure pier and originally extended much further out, years of violent storms having since taken their toll. Generations of Aber's students will have fond memories of a night out in the pier's nightclub, gratifyingly named 'Pier Pressure'.

Sweaty students are not the only creatures of the night to be found here, however. People flock from far and wide in winter to watch the famous starling murmuration as thousands of birds seek their communal night-time roosts at dusk before settling to roost on the girders below the pier buildings, and then leave together at dawn.

From here you'll have a full sweeping view along the promenade and the curve of the main bay. The town looks every inch a traditional Victorian bathing resort, and indeed if you were here in the 1800s you'd be greeted with the scene of Victorian ladies walking along the prom in their bustles underneath parasols, and rows of bathing machines along the shore. Slightly terrifying though they sound, bathing machines were simply wooden, or sometimes canvas, huts on wheels, where sea-goers could get changed and enter the sea while preserving their modesty. In addition, there were segregated parts of the beach where men and women could bathe separately, in accordance with the etiquette of the day.

A steep climb awaits to the top of Constitution Hill, 'Consti' as it is locally called. ❸ The route passes over the funicular railway – if you want to skip the first climb of the walk this could be an entertaining alternative to reach the top! Opened in 1896, the electric railway still takes visitors to the top of the hill where there is a café, play area and gift shops, as well as the fascinating yet now somewhat outdated Camera Obscura, the largest of its kind in the world, and one of the attractions of the Victorian resort. The Camera captures a panoramic image along the entire coastline and countryside. It's undoubtedly the perfect location for it – the views from Constitution Hill are phenomenal. From Strumble Head in Pembrokeshire, along the sweep of Cardigan Bay, to the mountains of Eryri and the hills and islands of Pen Llŷn, it is a breathtaking panorama. That's if you have any breath left after climbing the hill!

The route then hugs the coastline, heading north, before long dropping down to Clarach Bay. ❹ Although the huge caravan park dominates the scene here, the curve of golden sand and pebbles, with towering cliffs plunging into a sparkling sea, makes this a wonderful place to swim.

Walking northwards beyond Clarach Bay, the path is quiet; the rollercoaster of steep climbs and descents perhaps puts off many people. ❺ It is here that you can begin to appreciate the wilder side of this part of the coastline. As you approach Wallog, a prominent stone spit juts out into the sea for 6½ miles to a reef. This is Sarn Gynfelen, a stone causeway long associated with the legend of Cantre'r Gwaelod, the sunken kingdom of Welsh legend. Although the spit looks too uniform to be natural, it was in fact most probably a result of glacial deposits.

Ruled over by mythical figure Gwyddno Garanhir, the rich and fertile lost land of Cantre'r Gwaelod was, so they say, situated in the centre of what is now Cardigan Bay. Defended by sea walls, legend has it that one night the man charged with closing them became inebriated after attending a feast and forgot to close the defences. The tides flooded in and the land was lost forever. It is said that under certain conditions you can still hear the bells of Cantre'r Gwaelod from the coast here.

Descending next to the isolated 19th century mansion house at Wallog, you'll most likely have to share the beach only with oyster catchers, flocks of gulls and waders, or the odd inquisitive seal peering out at you from the water. Do be aware of the submerged rocks here, and take care not to trample the beds of the reef-building honeycomb worms that call this beach home. The steep crumbling cliffs of shale suffer frequent falls, so give them a wide berth too.

A steep climb ensues, perfect for warming up if your visit is on a cooler day. And if it isn't, then don't worry as there are two more opportunities to swim. ❻ A small, rocky cove near Pen y Graig caravan park, just before you begin the final climb to the war memorial is a lovely secluded and sheltered spot to swim. The amount of exposed rock and seaweed depends very much on recent sea conditions and the stage of the tide, though if you prefer a smoother option carry on to Borth.

Borth's beach is a long sweep of golden sand, and the southern end, known as Morfa Borth, is particularly lovely for swimming. ❼ It is popular with families and holiday makers and lifeguarded in summer. Borth's beach is more than just a good place for a swim though. As you make your way further along, you will come along the famous submerged forest, where remains of 5,000-year-old tree stumps and roots are revealed on a low tide. Human and animal footprints, including those of a four-year-old child, dated to 4,000 years ago, have been found in peat deposits buried under the sand. It is a humbling and poignant experience to watch the waves lap at the stumps of the trees and consider the passing of time. It takes a leap of the imagination to consider how this would have looked as a great forest rather than the vast beach it is today, but not so much to see how these intriguing coastal features could give rise to such rich legends of ancient sunken kingdoms.

DIRECTIONS

❶ If beginning in Borth, take the southbound train for Aberystwyth. Exit Aberystwyth Train Station and turn left. Walk along the road, crossing the first junction to continue ahead along Alexandra Road. At the roundabout, cross the road and turn right onto Chalybeate Street. Take the first left up Queen Street then at the junction cross the road to Princess Street and then cross the next onto Vulcan Street, following it down to arrive at South Beach.
0.4 miles

❷ From South Beach, follow the promenade north below the castle, past the Old College and past the pier to North Beach.
0.7 miles

❸ Continue along the promenade in the direction of Constitution Hill along Marine Terrace and Victoria Terrace. At the end of the road, turn right then take the left-hand turning signposted for the Wales Coast Path. Follow the path as it continues uphill, going over the bridges above the railway to reach the top of Constitution Hill.
0.7 miles

❹ Continue north along the coast path following it with the sea to your left. Descend towards the caravans, turning left to come out at the beach.
0.8 miles

❺ Cross the bridge over the stream at the far end and follow the clifftop path until it descends towards the large solitary mansion

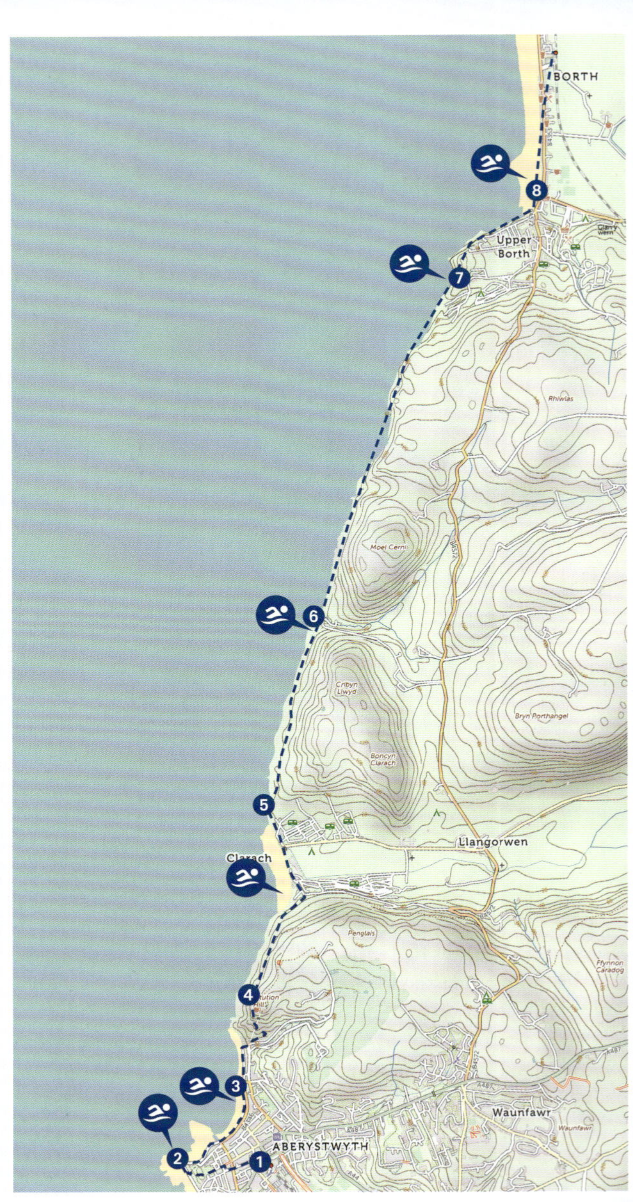

house at the bottom of the valley. Before you reach the house, turn left and walk past a lime kiln to get down onto the beach.
1.3 miles

❻ Return to the path, turn left to walk past the house and cross the footbridge before climbing back up onto the clifftops again. Continue along until you reach the next caravan park and the path descends to a rocky cove.
1.8 miles

❼ Take the steep set of steps up onto the clifftops next to the memorial. Follow this path around until it emerges on a lane next to some houses. Continue along Cliff Road to reach the beach.
0.7 miles

❽ Follow the main street or walk north along the beach and take the right-hand turning signposted Borth Station to return to the start.
0.8 miles

Walk 20

CWM EINION

At the northern extent of Ceredigion, and on the northernmost walk of this book, explore an enchanting forested river gorge with two fairytale pools to swim in. Follow in the footsteps of Wales' most celebrated 6th century bard and discover the remains of the industrial past.

There is a lot going on at the point where this walk begins. Whether you're arriving on the bus or by car, first of all, you're confronted with traffic racing along the busy A road between Aberystwyth and Machynlleth, but don't be put off. Secondly, the enormous building ahead of you can't fail to gain your attention.

The village descriptively named Furnace grew up around the iron works situated right on this spot. The charcoal-fired blast furnace dominates the area, and has done since the 1700s. The furnace was used to produce pig iron, and prior to this, there was a smelting works which, along with mines in the surrounding areas, produced enough silver for the Royal Mint to be established in nearby Aberystwyth. The Mint even moved here for a period in the 1600s when Cromwell seized Aberystwyth castle. As for the furnace's location, next to the rushing Afon Einion, this was ideal as the water was used to turn wheels and power the bellows which stoked the fires. Charcoal from the surrounding forests was plentiful, only the raw material had to be shipped in as there was no iron ore in the locality; it was more economical to transport the ore to an area with plentiful charcoal than to transport the charcoal to the iron ore. In later years, the furnace was used as a saw mill. The refurbished wheel on the exterior of the building is associated with this use.

All this makes for an unlikely location for a magical swimming spot. But that's exactly what can be found here, at the beginning

INFORMATION

This route is mostly on woodland paths, tracks and lanes. There are some muddy sections, and some paths can become overgrown by late summer. Nearest toilets at the RSPB reserve or at Cletwr.

DISTANCE: 3 miles, with 250 metres of ascent
TIME: 2 hours not including swims.
MAP: OS Explorer OL 23 Cadair Idris & Llyn Tegid
START & END POINT: Dyfi Furnace bridge. (SN 685 952). The bus stops here and there is a large free car park.
PUBLIC TRANSPORT: Trains and buses widely available to Aberystwyth and Machynlleth, and bus T28 between the two stops at Furnace bridge, where the walk begins
SWIMMING: Waterfall pool at Dyfi Furnace (SN 685 951) and pool higher up on the Einion at (SN 698 943)
PLACES OF INTEREST: Dyfi Furnace lime kilns and waterwheel, RSPB Ynys Hir (off route), Bedd Taliesin (off route)
REFRESHMENTS: The Cletwr community shop and café, a few miles south of Furnace (SY20 8PN, 01970 832113), is a wonderful place to stop for breakfasts, cakes, coffees and provisions. Y Llew Gwyn / The White Lion in Talybont (SY24 5ER, 01970 832245) is a great locals' pub which is welcoming to visitors and serves big pub food portions. If you want something really special and can afford the hefty price tag, then Ynyshir (SY20 8TA, 01654 781209), one of the best destination restaurants in Wales, can be found minutes away, though you'll need to book well in advance.

of the walk, less than a hundred metres from the roadside and the furnace building. As soon as you drop down to the level of the river, a magnificent amphitheatre of water, surrounded by steep gorge sides and overhung by a thick green canopy, instantly transports you to another world. A world where you can imagine that the land comes to life; see if you can make out the face in the rock drinking from the water as it cascades down into the pool below. As you'll be returning here at the end of the walk you can choose whether you want to swim before setting off or at the end, or if you enjoy this as much as I do, maybe twice!

The Afon Einion has its source on the slopes of Moel y Llyn, and travels only a short distance before reaching the Dyfi estuary at Ynys Hir. On its journey, it passes through one of the best examples of scarce and internationally important Tilio-Acerion woodland in Britain. ❷ This type of woodland is characterised by ash, wych elm and small-leaved lime trees, which are protected by the steep rocky gorge. Furthermore, more than one hundred and fifty species of liverworts and mosses, and one hundred and seventy species of lichen and ferns are present in the surrounding woodland. This environment is special enough to be one of four areas included in the Celtic Rainforests Wales conservation project. In spring the woodlands are carpeted with bluebells and violets, and in autumn the deciduous woodland turns to bronze. Even in winter the vibrant green mosses brighten up the dark, north-facing valley, known variously as Cwm Einion and Artists' Valley.

Climbing out of the woodland above the waterfall and emerging onto a track above the trees, the view to the north over the Dyfi estuary and the mountains of Eryri beyond, is spectacular. The village of Aberdyfi appears at the mouth of

the estuary, and below the wetlands of Ynys Hir stretch out. This RSPB reserve includes a number of habitats among its 800 hectares, with wetlands, reedbeds, saltmarsh, freshwater pools and oak woodlands. It's an important reserve for otters, grass snakes and many birds, notably waders and geese. The Greenland White-fronted Goose chooses to overwinter here, the only place where it does so in Wales. The reserve also has an enclosure populated by a family of beavers. Extinct in the wild, this native species helps to manage the birch and willow wetlands.

A little further up the estuary, the Dyfi Osprey Project has been working to support the recovery of ospreys in the Cors Dyfi Nature Reserve since 2009. Disappearing from the UK altogether in the early 1900s due to persecution, egg collectors and loss of habitat. Of approximately three hundred pairs now in Britain, five are now thought to be in Wales. All of the osprey chicks that have been born on the estuary are given the name of a Welsh river or lake; Einion was one of the first.

These important habitats all helped to secure UNESCO Biosphere Reserve status for the Dyfi

area. This designation recognises and supports the area's commitment to sustainably manage and develop healthy environments alongside its vibrant culture to encourage thriving communities and wildlife conservation. Of seven of these reserves in the UK, the Dyfi is the only one in Wales.

❸ The path skirts along the valley side before dropping down into the valley to the river again, and climbs to join the tiny lane which winds its way up the valley. After passing under a stand of sizeable Douglas Fir trees, the road comes close to the level of the river again, and a beautiful pool can be found below a set of cascades. ❹ Surrounded by ferns and beech trees, and with a gently sloping entry, it makes for a highly enjoyable swim. The valley can get busy during summer, and by busy, I mean a few walkers, cyclists and the odd car may drive past, but this doesn't detract from the overall magic of the setting. We had a wonderful swim here in the pouring rain, the rain bouncing onto the surface of the pool and pattering in the leaves all around – an enchanting experience.

❺ Our route returns from this point, but were you to continue up the valley you could explore further dipping spots in the river, and the abandoned Ystrad Einion mines. Silver, lead and copper were mined from the valley from the 18th century, the mines finally closing in 1902.

The valley is also home to a 75-acre private eco retreat, where guests encounter more beavers and a plantation of more than 20,000 native broadleaf trees, and can take courses in permaculture and self-sufficiency. Passing visitors are encouraged to pop by, and can tour the gardens and see the beavers for a small donation.

Our return route takes a high path through Coed Cerrig Mawr – Woodland of the Large Rocky Outcrop. ❻ In late summer this path can become overgrown; wearing shorts is ill-advised and a walking pole to whack through any vigorous bramble growth may be handy! Despite this, it is a beautiful route. Not far from here, just a couple of miles away in fact, lies a Bronze Age burial chamber dedicated to celebrated 6th century bard Taliesin. There is much doubt cast on the likelihood of Taliesin having actually been buried at the chamber, although it is known as Bedd Taliesin. His name is echoed in the landscape across this locality, suggesting a link with the renowned poet. His works, many pertaining to the ancient kings of Britain, are preserved in the 14th century Book of Taliesin, some of the oldest recorded poems in Cymraeg, Welsh. The manuscript is kept at the National Library of Wales in Aberystwyth. Perhaps the best known of the collection, Cad Goddeu – The Battle of the Trees, tells of legendary character Gwydion calling upon trees to fight a battle with him. As you continue through the woodland here perhaps the twisted and gnarled branches of the oaks and the knots of the ash will capture your imagination and conjure up images of the trees coming to life.

DIRECTIONS

1 On the opposite side of the river to the furnace building, a path leads down to the water's edge at the base of the waterfall. After a swim here, take the path leading steeply up into the trees on the same side of the river. Continue through the woods until you reach a lane.
0.1 miles

2 Walk out onto the lane, turn right and follow the lane as it bends left uphill. Shortly afterwards, a narrow path climbs to the right. Follow this uphill until you meet the next lane. Turn right and follow the lane to a track leading downhill to the right, signposted for the Wales Coast Path.
0.4 miles

3 Go down the track and through the gate at the bottom, below a cottage on the left. Bear right and cross the large footbridge. Turn right and follow the track all the way to the lane at the top.
0.3 miles

4 Turn left and continue on the lane until you reach the large pool on the left-hand side of the lane. After swimming here, turn and retrace your steps along the lane, taking a left turn onto a track. Bear slightly right on the track as it approaches some houses and then turn left, and immediately right onto a bridleway.
1.1 miles

5 Follow the path through the woodland, and turn right at the

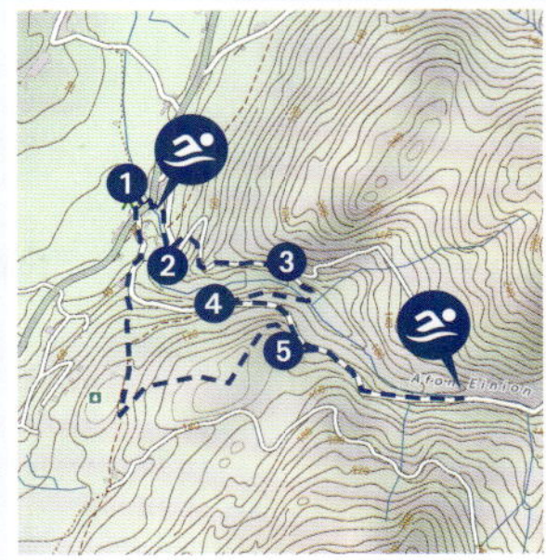

path junction. Turn left at the next junction to reach a well-defined track. Continue on this until you reach a path crossroads. Go straight ahead on the footpath heading directly downhill. Emerge onto a lane and turn left to follow it downhill, ending back at the furnace.
1 mile

Walk 21

DYFFRYN CASTELL AND LLYNNOED IEUAN

Follow in the footsteps of the Dragon's Back runners, and climb high above a fertile valley to the atmospheric Llynnoed Ieuan lakes to experience a true taste of the West Wales hinterlands. Bathe in the tranquillity of calm waters set amid the heathland, ethereal in the mist, or mellow under sunny skies.

The Dyffryn Castell Hotel began life as a Post House in the 1830s, beside the new turnpike road built through the valley. Post Houses kept horses and couriers to expedite communications, and to accommodate travellers on long journeys. During the 1800s, the Dyffryn Castell Hotel was a popular stop amongst the upper-class Romantic tourists. George Borrow, who wrote the travelogue 'Wild Wales', is counted amongst those who called in here, where he procured a guide to take him to explore Pumlumon to the north. He stayed in nearby Ponterwyd, at an inn now named The George Borrow after him. He wrote that on awaking, he found himself 'amongst wild, strange-looking hills, not, however, of any particular height'.

It is amongst these same hills, which Borrow would no doubt find even stranger-looking today, with the vast plantation forests and wind turbines, that this route is set. Our route begins in the lush, flat-bottomed valley which gave its name to the Dyffryn Castell hotel. Not very much at all is known about the 'castle' for which the river and the valley was named (Dyffryn means 'Valley'), but a nearby blink-and-you-miss-it earthwork, referred to as Llys Arthur – Arthur's Court – is the most likely source. The origin of the 'Llys' is unclear, but it is perhaps linked to the larger and slightly better-preserved Caer Gaer Roman fort to the east, which may have been adapted and altered during the medieval period.

INFORMATION

On good tracks to begin with, the route climbs for 320 metres. At the top you'll encounter very boggy and rough ground, with an increasingly faint path. The ability to take and follow a compass bearing and cross pathless terrain is important for the section between the two lakes, though you can opt to miss the second lake out. Swims are in cold, remote lakes.

DISTANCE: 3 miles
TIME: 2 hours not including swims
MAP: OS Explorer 213 Aberystwyth and Cwm Rheidol
START & END POINT: Parking area opposite the former Dyffryn Castell Hotel (SY23 3LB). If the inn ever reopens you may have to find alternative parking. Public transport: The X47 bus travels stops in Ponterwyd, from where you can follow the Cambrian Way for less than two miles to meet the route. Trains and buses connect with the bus at Aberystwyth and Llandrindod Wells.
SWIMMING: Lake swims at (SN 795 812), (SN 799 814) and (SN 795 817)
PLACES OF INTEREST: Castell lead mine (just off route), Llys Arthur (off route).
REFRESHMENTS: The George Borrow Inn (SY23 3AD, 01970 890230), in Ponterwyd is an historic Inn with a roaring fire, and good pub food overlooking some spectacular sections of gorge on the Rheidol. Further afield the Red Kite café (SY23 3AB, 01970 890340) is good for breakfasts, pies and burgers – popular with bikers and for classic car meets. Otherwise head to Pontarfynach for the Hafod Hotel (SY23 3JL, 01970 890232).

In later times, mining was carried out in the valley. In the 1700s mining for sphalerite, a zinc ore, was carried out at Castell mine. Later, lead and a small amount of copper were also mined here. Many traces of the mine are discernible in the valley, not least the large crusher house dating back to the late 1800s. A waterwheel drove machinery to crush the ore to separate the metals from the rock. Water was sourced from lakes high up on the hilltops and taken to the mines via a series of leats, channels through which the water was diverted.

A quick, easy walk through the lush valley floor and across the Afon Castell leads you to a solitary farm, Fagwr Fawr, centuries-old. ❷ Past the farm a steep climb ensues, easing the way up onto the hillside. As you climb, the views – should you be lucky enough to visit on a clear day – are far-reaching. Most times the only other souls you'll see around here are the sheep, and perhaps the farmer. Not so, though, if you happen to time your visit to coincide with the annual Dragon's Back race, when hundreds of runners stop here for the night in a large camp set up as their overnight stop. This is after running 40 miles over Cader Idris and Pumlumon on day three of the north-to-south race from Conwy to Cardiff, one of the world's toughest mountain races. Day four begins with the same steep climb that you are now on and, if you are finding it hard going, console yourself with the fact that most of the runners walk up this track too.

On a clear day, the summit of Pumlumon will be visible behind as you leave the track and climb higher towards the plateau. ❸ The uplands here all form part of the Elenydd Special Area of Conservation. More locally, the area around Llynnoed Ieuan is a designated Site of Special Scientific Interest. This is recognised as a good example of blanket mire, commonly referred to as blanket bog, and subalpine heath, characterised by the presence of bell heather and bilberries. ❹ The lakes themselves are thought to have been dammed some time during the 1800s in association with the now-abandoned mines at Castell, and Nantycreuau further south.

Another reason for the conservation designation of the lakes is, in technical terms, their 'oligotrophic' nature. Essentially this means they are nutrient-poor, typically stony-bottomed, and are mildly acidic. Specialised plants found here include shoreweed, quillwort, water starwort, water lobelia and water plantain, to name a few. These species are at risk from invasive species and alterations to the water's acidity, so when swimming here the usual guidance is important: to check, clean and dry your swimwear, or even better, having a cheeky skinny dip instead. Even sunscreen and other skin or hair products could have an impact, so this is worth considering.

We come first to the largest of the three lakes which are collectively named Llynnoed Ieuan, Ieuan's lakes. Ieuan is a common man's name in Welsh, pronounced y-ey-an. I've been unable to find out who exactly Ieuan is or was, and why the lakes are named after him. We had great fun on our walk coming up with a few different stories behind the name, but in all likelihood, the Ieuan in question was probably the landowner. The first lake's southern shore offers a gentle entry to the water, with a flat grassy bank perfect for changing. ❺ The lake is relatively shallow, around five metres at its deepest, so is not as cold as some others at this altitude. A swim here in the mist is utterly enchanting; you feel as though the world could have ended and you'd never know.

For a second swim, you have a choice. If you're confident with compass bearings, you can circumnavigate the lake to its eastern shore then simply take a bearing across to the next lake. ❻ There is no easy way to get between them, and you'll have to navigate bog and heather no matter which way you choose, but the higher ground at the southern end of the lake may keep your feet relatively drier. Tread gently here, especially during bird nesting season when there may be ground nesting birds present. If you go with this option, you can have a second swim in the middle of the three lakes, overlooked by steep banks and forestry at the far end. This lake is slightly more vegetated and softer underfoot at some points; avoid stirring up the silt if you can – a shallow swoosh across the surface can help this. This lake feels even wilder; you may be accompanied by the honking of wild geese and spot ripples on the water, giving away the presence of fish within. Beyond, the sense of wilderness is interrupted by plantation forestry and the Cefn Croes Wind Farm. Once the UK's largest onshore wind farm, the turbines here produce enough power for 37,000 homes.

The third and furthest lake is not worth the effort to reach, unless you want to lose a battle with the mire and end up being unearthed as a bog body by future archaeologists! Follow a back bearing to the first lake, where you could have a third swim at the other end. ❼ Continue around to the north of

the lake; a stony, gently sloping beach at the far end offers an easy entry into and out of the crystal-clear water, and a great place to picnic and sunbathe, or change quickly and easily in less pleasant weather.

Completing the loop around the lake, the views from the descent back on the same track are breathtaking, with the shape of the hills contrasting in layers ahead. ❽ You can understand why people feel protective over this landscape. A proposal to develop a further windfarm on the hills surrounding Pumlumon to the north has been faced with strong opposition; the 'No Pylons', 'No Turbines', and the wider campaign against perceived land-grabbing 'Nid yw Cymru ar Werth' – Wales Is Not for Sale – slogans can be frequently seen on placards dotted around the countryside. One of the main opponents, the Cambrian Mountains Society, is particularly concerned about the impact on this treasured landscape and the communities. This is only the latest battle between the demand for resources such as water, energy and minerals, the need to mitigate climate change, and consideration for the communities, heritage, language and landscapes which has been ongoing in mid-Wales for centuries, at the frontiers of mines, reservoirs, forestry, farmland and even the skyline.

DIRECTIONS

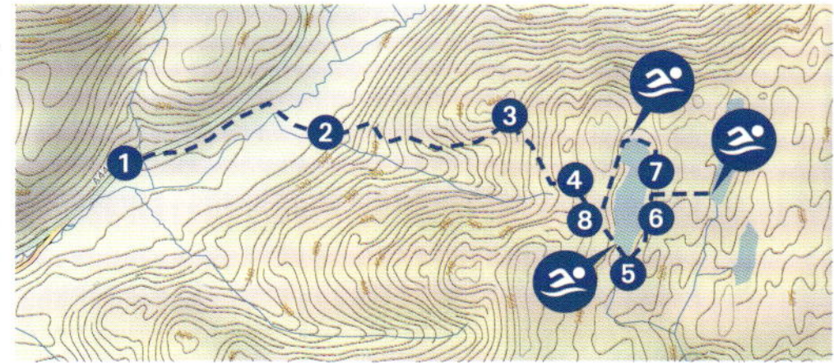

❶ Looking at the old Dyffryn Castell Hotel from the opposite side of the road, turn right and walk along the road which crosses a stream, for a short distance to a lane leading off to the right. Turn down the lane, go over the cattle grid and continue on the lane, until you reach a driveway on the right signposted Fagwr Fawr. Turn down the driveway to the farm.
0.5 miles

❷ Go through both gates, between the barns. Take a left on the track going uphill. Ignore tracks branching off to the left. Continue steeply uphill until you reach a gate and a stile on your right.
0.6 miles

❸ Cross the stile, following a grassy, muddy path uphill, bearing left as the ground opens up to the right and the path flattens. Cross a small ditch and bear right, climbing up on to the higher ground on a now-faint path, which passes a small pond to your left.
0.3 miles

❹ From the pond, continue south-east to reach the southern tip of the lake. The path is now very faint and may not be at all discernible, so in poor visibility you may want to take a bearing from the pond. Tip: If you bear slightly north of the southern tip then you're less likely to miss it.
0.2 miles

❺ Continue anti-clockwise around the lake, with the water on your left. A faint quad bike path circumnavigates the lake which makes for slightly easier walking, otherwise stick to the high ground and keep the lake in close sight to avoid going wrong.
0.2 miles

❻ If you'd like to visit the second lake, take a direct east bearing when you are approximately halfway along the eastern length of the first lake, to reach the southern edge of the second lake. After swimming, return to the lake on an opposite (west) bearing, or in good weather just retrace your steps to the higher ground.
0.3 miles

❼ Continue around the first lake on the high ground with the water close on your left. As you approach the northern end of the lake, drop down on a narrow path towards the northern shore. After swimming here, continue on a narrow path around the lake, heading south, then bearing away from the lake once you've climbed up to the high ground, south-west. There is a narrow path which should bring you back alongside the pond seen earlier.
0.4 miles

❽ Retrace your earlier steps, descending on the path to the north, crossing the stile then continuing back downhill on the track, through the farmyard and back along the lane to the Dyffryn Castell.
1.5 miles

Walk 22

CWM RHEIDOL

Wander through woodland and climb high up onto the hillside for far-reaching views over Cwm Rheidol, surely one of the most beautiful valleys in the region. Swim in the river accompanied by birdsong and the echoes of the steam train.

The Rheidol valley with its steep wooded hillsides, lush flood plain and snaking river, narrowing to a rocky gorge with waterfalls tumbling through as you travel upstream, is a verdant vein into the heart of mid-west Wales. Its source is high on the slopes of Pumlumon (Plynlimon), mid-Wales' great mass of mountain, and it reaches the sea just 19 miles later at Aberystwyth, making it one of the steepest rivers for its short length in Wales.

Occupied since the Bronze Age and likely much further back, the valley, which once thronged with the activity of a heavy metal mining industry, is now a peaceful and serene place with a tight-knit community of agriculturalists, artists and creatives. The sleepy area comes to life in summer, with the magnificent Vale of Rheidol steam railway puffing through the valley from Aberystwyth, following the course of the river upstream to Pontarfynach (otherwise known as Devil's Bridge). It's a legacy of the freight trains from the mining era. A butterfly house and riding stables provide further entertainment for families, but it is the river crashing and winding through the valley which holds the most fascination.

The Afon Rheidol was much altered in the 1960s through a series of reservoirs. The first and highest, Nant y Moch, collects water from the mountain using aqueducts; this is then channelled into Dinas reservoir to a power plant. Dinas reservoir is also used as a fishery, stocked with brown and rainbow trout. From there it is linked to the Cwm Rheidol Power Station, which we'll pass during our walk. Combined, elements of the Cwm Rheidol hydroelectric scheme produce enough renewable energy to power 25,000 homes.

INFORMATION

Mixed terrain: expect mud, woodland tracks, steep slopes, fields, footbridges and stiles. The walk involves some climbing.

DISTANCE: 8 miles with 485 metres of ascent
TIME: 5 hours
MAP: OS Explorer 213 Aberystwyth and Cwm Rheidol
START & END POINT: Cwm Rheidol lead mine (SN 729 781, SY23 3NB). A few parking spaces are available here. There is additional parking near the reservoir and power plant to join the route there.
PUBLIC TRANSPORT: Trains and buses widely available to Aberystwyth. The X47 bus service which connects Llandrindod Wells and Aberystwyth has stops at Capel Bangor (Penllwyn) and Goginan which are both about 1½ miles from the route. Another, more costly but scenic, option would be to take the Vale of Rheidol steam train which is a tourist service between Aberystwyth and Devil's Bridge, and has stops just off the route.
SWIMMING: Waterfall (SN 728 781), and a large river pool below the footbridge (SN 681 792)
PLACES OF INTEREST: Lead mine ruins, Rheidol Falls (no swimming), reservoir & hydropower plant, Tan-y-Ffordd hillfort
REFRESHMENTS: Statkraft café, Rheidol Vale reservoir visitor centre (SY23 3NB, 01970 880 667). In Devil's Bridge: Two Hoots Tea Room at the train station is a great spot for walkers (SY23 3JL, 07779 450735) or the Hafod Inn (SY23 3JL, 01970 890232).

Our walk begins at the end of the sleepy lane on the northern banks of the river near disused lead mine ruins, where there is space for a few cars to park. Bear in mind there may be no space here during busy summer periods and the driveways leading to people's houses are not for parking in. As an alternative, park at the visitor centre which is halfway through the walk and join it there.

Mining was carried out throughout the valley from the 17th century until World War I. Lead, zinc, copper and marcasite (white iron pyrite) were mined here under lax environmental controls. Because the law releases any mining entity carrying out their activities up to 1999 from being responsible for environmental damage, for years the waters of the Rheidol were heavily polluted by toxic substances arising from the destabilisation of the metals being extracted. The river's biodiversity was obliterated by the pollution, and the Rheidol was considered a dead river. Today, a variety of methods including settling ponds, reed beds and filters, help reduce the pollution entering the river and many people enjoy swimming at various points along its course.

Our first swim is at a beautiful waterfall where there is a stony bank below some old mine buildings, and a deep pool in the water. Be aware of large submerged rocks here and a sometimes very strong flow. Use good judgement before entering. This is an enchanting place to swim. Salmon and wild trout inhabit the river, in vulnerable numbers, so tread gently on the river bed. Otters have returned here, and a heron accompanied us just upstream of the waterfall during our swim. If you are parked here, you can always leave this swim until last and enjoy the dark green of the water contrasted with the sun kissing the top of the trees as it dips below the hill.

From the river there is a steep walk up through forestry land. At first this is planted coniferous forest where you may hear the sound of goldcrests singing at a decibel level that belies their tiny size. Soon, the conifers give way to the deciduous forest of Coed Simdde lwyd. Meaning 'Wood of the Grey Chimney' the name may relate to charcoal burning in the area between the 16th and 18th centuries. This woodland is managed by the Wildlife Trust and is characterised by sessile oak, with ferns, mosses and liverworts. Heather and bilberry carpet the woodland floor, and jays, redstart, pied flycatchers and wood warblers are some of the bird species you may be lucky enough to spot. This ancient upland oak woodland is a National Nature Reserve, Site of Special Scientific Interest and forms part of the Rheidol Woods and Gorges Special Area of Conservation.

The woodland is over far too soon. We emerge into a very boggy field before reaching the gloriously solid country lane! There is very little traffic along here, and the views over the surrounding countryside, now that we have climbed high out of the gorge, are expansive, rolling hillsides like a crumpled green patchwork blanket. We join a cycle route that begins to descend on a track through fields and passes a distinct mound in the woodland to the left; this is the remains of the Iron Age Tan-Y-Ffordd hillfort.

Reaching the lane at river level again, you soon see a footbridge over the river on your left. On the other side of the bridge there is a gently sloping entrance into the calmer water on the inside of the river meander. We had fun paddling upstream to the top of the meander, then swimming out into the current and swooshing downstream underneath the bridge, then swimming harder to escape the current back onto the bank. It's a

gorgeous spot surrounded by oak trees and views up the valley. After swimming, walk, following the river upstream, but don't be tempted to swim any further past the meander; there are some vicious looking metal contraptions in the water at many locations. The pretty village of Aberffrwd is situated just downstream of the mighty Cwm Rheidol reservoir and dam. Again, not a place for swimming due to all of the machinery and currents present. It is scenic and peaceful despite being home to the largest power plant of its kind in Wales. If you're joining the route from the visitor centre this is where you'll arrive. The dam here is used to control the flow of water to help prevent flooding downstream at Aberystwyth.

Soon after the reservoir is the pretty Rheidol Vale Falls, a favourite with tourists past and present. There are a couple of picnic benches here so it's a great place to take a break, though again, not a place to swim due to the lack of a safe exit as well as weirs in the water.

The walk continues through fields with more remains of mining works. The steam trains run above, their whistles echoing around the valley. Back into deciduous woodland, often carpeted with bluebells and violets in spring, rare species such as Wilson's filmy fern, and yellow cow-wheat thrive here. This beautiful woodland is a sanctuary for mammals too: otters, pine martens, polecats and badgers are all at home here, though are elusive. In 2015 twenty pine martens were released by the Vincent Wildlife Trust to boost the fragile population in the valley.

The walk finishes up descending towards the river once again, crossing a footbridge over a narrow rocky gorge section of the river, and coming out onto the lane just a short distance from the start.

DIRECTIONS

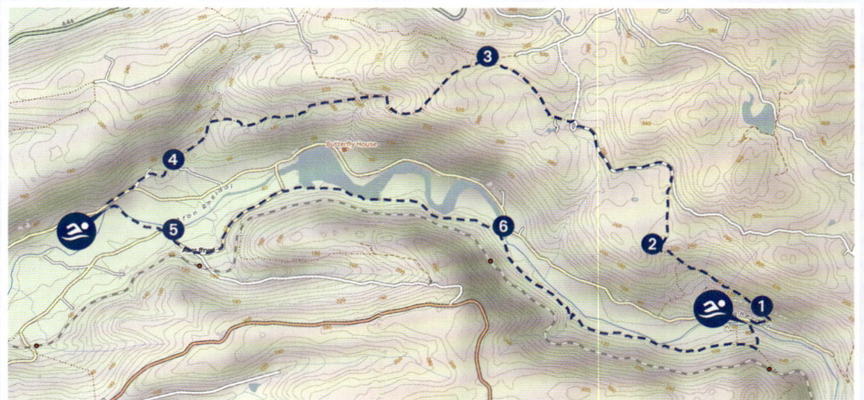

❶ Begin at the waterfall close to the old mines near the end of the road on this side of the valley. After swimming, return to the road and look for a track immediately on your right. The track bends left and climbs up through woodland, until you reach a house. Go behind the house, continuing uphill and into the Coed Simdde Llwyd National Nature Reserve. Continue climbing steeply through the woods until you reach a gate into a field.
0.7 miles

❷ Walk through the centre of the field, keeping to the right of the left boundary to avoid the worst of the bogginess. Aim for the top left point of the field to the left of the house. Join a track which passes through the farm before joining the lane and turning left. Continue on the lane until it becomes a track, passing through farm buildings then reaching a crossroads. Take the centre track, ahead, and continue on the track ignoring paths off to the left, until you reach the house Pen-rhiwlas.
1.5 miles

❸ Here the track splits and on the right joins a lane. Take the track heading south-west, on the left. The track splits once again at a house in the trees. Continue on the lower track, heading left, but ignore the footpath which soon joins in from the left and keep to the track, as it heads through an avenue of trees. Follow the track downhill which can be extremely muddy, and hop a small stream (which may be dry after no rain) next to a large white house. Soon you'll reach the road.
2 miles

❹ Turn right on the road and very soon look for a footpath heading towards the river. Cross the bridge and turn left to reach the stony river bank. After swimming, return back to the path and turn left, keeping the river to your left, until you reach a lane.
0.4 miles

❺ Turn left on the lane, and walk through the village of Aberffrwd. Continue on the lane all the way to the Rheidol Vale Reservoir. Join a track into the trees up ahead, keeping the reservoir, then river, on your left. Take a left fork in the path to reach Rheidol Falls.
1.8 miles

❻ Follow the path alongside the river, then take a right up behind the disused mine buildings to reach a gate onto a path that runs alongside the woodland. Continue with the fence line on your left, and when the path turns to head uphill, continue ahead on a path not marked on the OS map. Turn left, cross the stile on your left and walk downhill to reach a footbridge over the river. Cross the footbridge and turn right up the lane to return to the start.
1.6 miles

Walk 23

PONTARFYNACH

A quiet walk along the upper Mynach river, into deep countryside. Swim in an enchanting section of gorge next to a forgotten mill, and enjoy lazy, laidback river dips surrounded by moorland, forests and hillsides. Then return to the village to learn the legend of the Devil's Bridge.

Pontarfynach, 'Bridge over the Monk's River', or as it is widely known in English, Devil's Bridge, has been attracting visitors since the 18th century, thanks to the spectacular gorge through which the Mynach river roars, and the three-tiered bridge which spans it. The legend of how the bridge was first created gave rise to the English name of the village. The tale goes that an old lady lost her cow on the other side of the river and needed to cross. The devil appeared and offered that he would build a bridge in return for the first living creature to cross it. The lady returned a short while later and found that the bridge had been built. Watching and waiting, the devil was nevertheless outwitted by the old woman: she threw a loaf of bread across the river, and her dog chased it, becoming the first living creature to cross the bridge, so that the woman escaped the clutches of the devil. Spare a thought for the poor dog in this tale!

There are records of the river being bridged here since medieval times. Gerallt Cymro – Gerald of Wales – wrote about crossing a wooden bridge during his travels here in the 12th century. The lowest bridge is thought to date to the medieval period, and was perhaps constructed by the monks of Strata Florida Abbey (see Walk 24) to ease the way to the abbey from the nearby church at Ysbyty Cynfin. A second bridge, flatter in profile, was built in the 1700s. The current road bridge was built in 1901. Unfortunately, you're unable to see the stacked bridges from above or to view

INFORMATION

Mostly good paths and tracks, but there are areas that get overgrown with bracken and nettles in summer, and some muddy and boggy sections.

DISTANCE: 5 miles
TIME: 3 hours excluding swims
MAP: OS Explorer 213 Aberystwyth and Cwm Rheidol
START & END POINT: Hafod Hotel, Pontarfynach (Devil's Bridge) (SN 741 770, SY23 3JL). Parking can be tricky, but there's a car park and toilets at the railway; check opening and closing times. On weekends you could park by the school, being mindful of residents.
PUBLIC TRANSPORT: Many buses and trains go to Aberystwyth, then a taxi to Pontarfynach (Devil's Bridge). There is a tourist steam train service through the Rheidol Vale from Aberystwyth but it's not convenient for this walk unless you were to stay overnight in the village.
SWIMMING: River gorge (SN 749 765) and pools in river (SN 767 773, SN 767 774 and SN 769 776)
PLACES OF INTEREST: Devil's Bridge and Mynach Falls (no swimming), Nant Syddion bothy (a short diversion)
REFRESHMENTS: The Two Hoots Tea Room (SY23 3JL, 07779 450735) at the Rheidol Vale Railway terminus has delicious tea and Welsh cakes or bara brith, also cooked breakfasts and paninis. Don't miss the Hafod Hotel (SY23 3JL, 01970 890232) for a post-walk drink on the terrace overlooking the valley, with gastro pub food. Woodlands Caravan Site also has a very good tea room and shop for provisions (SY23 3JW, 01970 890423).

the waterfalls unless you pay your coins into the turnstile to access the fenced-off gorge.

Hafod was built as a lavish lodge for Thomas Johnes, Member of Parliament for Cardigan and scholar of Eton and Jesus College Oxford, in the 1780s. Many high-profile visitors were attracted to visit the estate including JMW Turner, whose detailed watercolour 'Hafod' depicts the grandeur of the house. According to John Feltham, author of 'A Guide to All the Watering and Sea Bathing Places', the property was substantially damaged by fire in 1807, and it was 'impossible to calculate the loss which literature has sustained in this conflagration, which consumed many rare and expensive books, a collection of Welsh manuscripts and other articles impossible to be replaced'. After the fire, Johnes turned to agriculture and planted half a million trees across his estate.

Hafod still continues to draw tourists to this day, as a now well-respected hotel and pub. The Welsh-language TV noir series Y Gwyll, or Hinterland as it was internationally known, featured the hotel and the surrounding Cambrian Mountains.

Leaving Pontarfynach behind for now, our route begins by following the lane around the southern edge of the Devil's Bridge gorge, before turning onto a track which follows the river valley upstream. ❷ This quiet track is part of the descriptive, yet not very catchily titled 'Borth to Devil's Bridge to Pontrhydfendigaid Trail'. As you progress along the valley the views open out. Forestry plantations, and more specifically clear felling, has taken its toll on the landscape here, a reminder that this part of Wales has been for decades, and is often still treated as no more than a commodity. There is beauty to be found in the curves of the hillsides, the meadows filled with marsh orchids and bog asphodel, and in the water which tumbles through

the valley in an altogether gentler fashion than the roaring cascades further downstream.

There are several spots to get into the river for a dip as the path runs alongside it. ❸ Banks vegetated with rowan, willow, heather and the odd escapee conifer overlook the peaty waters and rocky river bed. Joined by wagtails, dippers and dragonflies, you submerge and feel the water wash away all your cares. Soon after the first swim, there is another deep spot on a river bend, then yet another as the river is joined by the Afon Myherin. As the river swings eastwards, a narrow mini gorge cuts through the rocks below a footbridge, with cascades flowing into it giving you another place to plunge. ❹

Moving away from the river, the route crosses a large open meadow before descending to cross a minor stream once more, and join a forestry

track. 5 Were you to continue north on this track, instead of south, you'd reach the Nant Syddion bothy, a disused farmhouse with a tragic past which now provides walkers with a shelter for the night. One look through the visitor book may make you turn on your heels and head straight back out the door however, as tales of hauntings abound in the accounts of those who have braved an overnight stay. Behind the ghost stories is a tragic tale of the fate of the Hughes family who lived here, and the first recorded quadruplets to be born in Wales. Out of respect for the real lives affected, and because the tale is far too sad to mar the delights of this chapter, I will leave it to you to read elsewhere on what happened to them if you're curious.

6 The route now returns back in the direction of Pontarfynach, tracing the river downstream on the opposite side of the valley, along a forest track, into woodland and climbing high up on a bracken-clad path. 7 As you reach the top of the climb, the views back over the valley below and over to Cwm Rheidol and beyond are worth pausing to take in.

The descent takes you through a sparse oak woodland, and past a caravan park, but then turns south back towards the Mynach. 8 Dropping down into the trees, you'll reach an unexpected and enchanting section of gorge hidden away next to the ruins of an old mill. Crossing the footbridge high above, the sun filters through the trees to dapple the waters below. The beautifully clear river carves through moss-laden rocks before heading off downstream where it will soon plunge down the face of the famous falls. Needless to say, you would not want to get swept downstream, so carefully judge the flow and force of the water, and your safe exit, before deciding whether to swim.

Access isn't especially easy, and involves a short scramble through undergrowth and negotiating some low tree branches to reach rocks and gravel at the river's edge, from where you can ease yourself in. But it is absolutely worth getting leaves stuck in your hair and a few bramble scratches. Entering below the bridge, swimming upstream underneath it to another pool and narrow section of gorge, then swooshing back down, is especially fun. The deep section of gorge offers opportunity for jumps, but the usual cautions apply here; at the time of my visit there was a tree trunk submerged across the river which needed to be carefully avoided.

9 It is difficult to drag yourself away from this spot, but knowing that only a short section of track and road lies between you and a well-earned drink with a view at the Hafod, should spur you on to the end of the walk.

DIRECTIONS

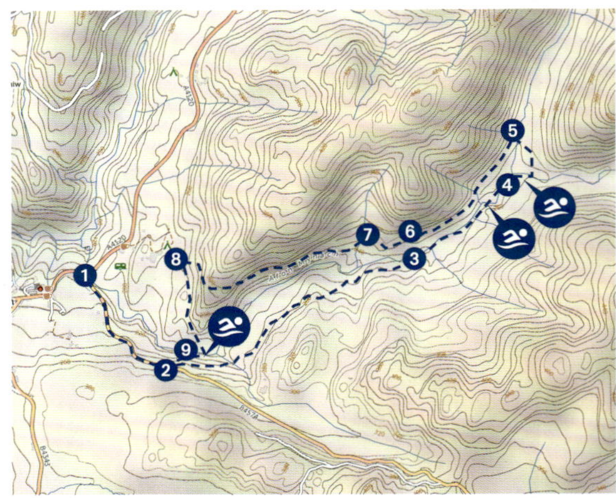

❶ From the Hafod Hotel, walk along the B-road signposted for Cwmystwyth and Hafod. Note that this is a narrow lane and vehicles do sometimes travel fast along this road, so keep your wits about you. Take the first track on the left, after the pink house on your right. As an alternative on weekends there are spaces for a few cars near the school, and if you wanted to cut out the road section you could take the Borth to Devils Bridge to Pontrhydfendigaid Trail heading east to join our route, coming out at the entrance to the track.
0.5 miles

❷ Walk down the track, and follow the diversion around the house downhill. Cross a stream, go through a gate, then continue along the track through fields. It becomes boggy for a section, continue ahead to a stone wall, then through another field to reach a gate in the far-left hand corner, nearest the river.
1.1 miles

❸ Follow the track alongside the river. When you reach a gate, with trees behind the fence to your right, you can drop down behind the post at the start of the fence on the left to a section of the river which has a couple of deep pools to swim. Continue back on the track, still following the river upstream, round a bend where there is another deep pool in the river. Continue further along the path and on the corner where another stream comes in on the opposite side, near an old stone construction, a trail leads down into the river making for another good swim spot.
0.6 miles

❹ Follow the path as it bends east – the OS map is out of date – and briefly into the conifer trees before turning left and crossing a footbridge below a set of cascades. You could also have a dip off the rocks below the bridge. Climb up from the bridge heading towards the conifer trees and track but then veer left across the meadow, heading down towards a stream and footbridge.
0.3 miles

❺ Cross the footbridge and climb the steps on the other side to reach the forestry track. Turn left and follow the track down until you reach a stile on the left; it is quite overgrown and easy to miss – if you reach the locked forestry gate you've gone too far.
0.6 miles

❻ Cross the stile then descend through trees to an old track between stone walls, past some derelict stone buildings and alongside a more modern house. Join a grassier track, then look out for a stile up on your right, which is also quite overgrown, into the conifer plantation.
0.3 miles

❼ Follow the clear path as it climbs upwards through the conifer plantation, and comes out onto open hillside. There is a path climbing up along the hillside but it can be very overgrown with bracken during the summer – keep going, heading uphill until you come to a grassier shoulder and marker posts to follow, going west. The path veers north-west

and descends into oak woodland and through a field, coming out at a junction of paths.
0.7 miles

❽ Turn left and follow the track along the top of a field, to a gate. If the gate on the right of way is locked shut, you will have to climb it to get into the field, then follow the path into the trees, down towards a footbridge. Cross the footbridge then turn right and climb down a short way to the river below.
0.4 miles

❾ Return to the path and turn right, climbing uphill. When you reach the track at the top, turn right and return to the road. Either turn right and follow the road back to the Hafod Hotel, or go straight over to take the path back towards the school.
0.6 miles

Walk 24

TEIFI POOLS AND CLAERDDU

Explore the expanse of the Elenydd uplands at the Teifi Pools, lakes galore glittering at the source of the River Teifi, at the geographical centre of Wales. Opt to extend your trip for an overnight stay in the remote Claerddu Bothy, and learn about the monks and shepherds that once roamed this land, and a giant too!

The solitude-seeking Cistercians chose beautiful, remote and serene valleys for their early medieval abbeys, and Ystrad Fflur – the Valley of Flowers – home to Strata Florida Abbey, is no exception. Today a popular visitor attraction, place of pilgrimage and important monument in Welsh history, this ruined relic lies in the same valley as our route begins. It was established by the Norman lord Robert FitzStephen in the early 12th century, but was soon after captured by the unstoppable Rhys ap Gruffudd, Prince of Deheubarth. With his realm covering vast swathes of western and central Wales, the Abbey was further endowed and relocated two miles up the valley from its original position which must have proved unsuitable for the new, larger construction.

It flourished during the later 12th century under Lord Rhys, its importance is reflected in the number of notable burials here, including eleven princes from the house of Dinefwr, the long-standing rulers of Deheubarth, and of renowned medieval poet Dafydd ap Gwilym. Another, later poet, T Gwynn Jones, paid homage to the Abbey in his early 20th century popular Welsh Poem 'Ystrad Fflur' (Strata Florida), written in traditional cynghanedd style.

It is worth calling in to visit the Abbey to see the ancient yews and marvel at what remains of the ornate medieval construction, either on your way to the walk or on the way back, as from any approach you will be passing the Abbey's entrance.

INFORMATION

Good paths, lanes and tracks make up the bulk of the route, but there is a fair amount of pathless bog-hopping to be negotiated in the middle part of the walk.

DISTANCE: 10 miles
TIME: 6 hours – but you could make two very leisurely days of it by splitting the route with an overnight in Claerddu Bothy.
MAPS: OS Explorer 187 Llandovery and 213 Aberystwyth and Cwm Rheidol
START & END POINT: Cwm Egnant car park (SN 770 655); from Strata Florida Abbey (SY25 6ES) take the no-through road to the left of the graveyard and follow it up to the parking area.
PUBLIC TRANSPORT: The T21 bus stops at Pontrhydfendigaid and Ffair Rhos, a few miles' walk from the route. This bus connects to onward buses and trains in Aberystwyth.
SWIMMING: Claerddu waterfall pool dip (SN 792 690), lake swims at Llyn Fyrddon Fach and Llyn Fyrddon Fawr (SN 797 700 and SN 801 706). Additional swims at Llyn y Gorlan and Llyn Hir (SN 786 670 and SN 789 677)
PLACES OF INTEREST: Claerddu Bothy, Strata Florida Abbey (nearby), the geographical centre of Wales
REFRESHMENTS: The café at Strata Florida Abbey (SY25 6ES) is a great spot right in the Abbey grounds for teas, coffees and cake. Otherwise you'll need to head to Ffair Rhos or Pontrhydfendigaid where you'll find local pubs at the Teifi Inn (SY25 6BP, 01974 831849) and the Red Lion Hotel (SY25 6BH, 01974 831010).

The walk begins from higher up in the valley, but below Cwm Egnant, which you'll have the pleasure of returning to on your descent from the pools later on. First, skirting round the hillside, on a narrow path through shoulder-high bracken in summer, the loveliness of this tranquil valley cannot be overstated. ❷ Red kites wheel overhead and foxgloves decorate the grassy slopes of the hillside. A track winds uphill through farmland, with the verdant rolling countryside stretching out below.

Leaving the tamer lowland farms behind, you'll reach open hillside where sheep graze freely. ❸ Here you enter the broad sweep of the Elenydd uplands. Cotton grass and asphodel, which has beautiful yellow flowers in summer and flame-red stalks once the flowers have died off, are tell-tale giveaways of the boggy ground that you'll negotiate as you climb through the valley.

All at once, you'll emerge next to the Llyn Teifi dam, the source of West Wales' longest river, where it begins its 76-mile journey to the sea. Llyn Teifi is the largest of the Teifi Pools - the name given to the collective of upland lakes and reservoirs here - and deep. It has been revered for its fish, including wild brown trout, for centuries. Indeed, the lakes here provided a good supply of fish for the Abbey during the medieval period. The only recreation on Llyn Teifi is paid for by anglers and, as is the policy at all of Welsh Water's reservoirs, no swimming is permitted. Which is a shame, because away from the dams it would make for a wonderful swim.

Climbing up away from Llyn Teifi, you'll walk on a narrow band of rough, high ground known as Graig Felen. ❹ From here you could choose to drop down to Llyn y Gorlan to the south-east if you want to swim there. Though there is no easy path, you should be able to pick your way down to Llyn y Gorlan and back up over the tussocky slopes, clad with bilberries and heather. Llyn Hir is more easily accessed from a track as you descend from the broad ridge. These glistening lakes are not reservoirs, but are used as fishing lakes, so being respectful and keeping your distance from anyone fishing here should mean you are able to enjoy basking in the clear water and sunbathing on the grassy shores on a warm day or, more likely, a bracing swim and jumping around to warm up afterwards, an altogether more exhilarating experience!

Briefly, our route crosses paths with the ancient road known as the 'Monks Trod', which connected Strata Florida Abbey with Abbey Cwmhir in the upper Wye Valley. Undoubtedly quite an undertaking to construct, today it is a peaceful, lonely route across this vast Welsh 'wilderness', interrupted only by the odd party of scrambler bikes who appear to derive great enjoyment from tearing up the ground of this byway.

After a short section on the track, turning into a tarmacked reservoir road, you'll turn off towards Claerddu Bothy. Maintained by the Elan Valley Trust, this simple shelter is a stripped-back farmhouse abandoned as such in the 20th century. It contains only two small downstairs rooms with a fire place, bare-bones furniture, and two upstairs rooms with large sleeping platforms. It's popular with those seeking to spend a night out in the remoteness of the Cambrian Mountains. Bothies are run on goodwill, with a general code of conduct being to respect the surroundings: leave no trace and bring in your own firewood from a sustainable source – which means not cutting down surrounding trees (which don't burn anyway!) There is no running water here, but remarkably there is an outside flushing loo – pure luxury by bothy standards. The Teifi Pools are designated as a Dark Sky Discovery Site, so if you do decide to stay and are lucky enough to have clear skies, you're in no better place to appreciate the stars. You never know who you may meet in a bothy; you could have the entire place to yourself, or end up sharing it with a rowdy group, so be prepared for any eventuality. If you don't fancy an overnight here, it makes for a great lunch stop, to ponder on what life would have been like for the shepherds who once called this home.

Antiquarian John Leland visited Claerddu in the 1500s and his writing provides a remarkable account of life here during that time. He came across several hafodtai – seasonal farmhouses – and spoke to the shepherds. They took him to a nearby waterfall and told him the legend of a giant, Arthur, who washed his hands in the pool below. ❺ As we continue on our route, it feels very special to retrace these steps from hundreds of years ago to the same waterfall and swim in the very pool revered by the people inhabiting this place in the distant past.

From the waterfall we return to the bothy, where you have the option to make this a shorter walk by skipping forward to direction 7 to begin the return from here. The next part of the route is an exciting, if somewhat arduous out-and-back leg starting from, and returning to the bothy, for those who are feeling energetic and keen for more exploring and swims. ❻

This leg follows the Cambrian Way long distance trail northwards. You may need to use a compass in poor visibility. Climbing up from the bothy, the vast expanse of upland blanket bog stretches out, seemingly endlessly. Boggy and for the most part pathless, bring your best navigation skills. This is the geographical centre of Wales; the exact spot is pinpointed a few hundred metres north of our route, but you really do get the feeling of being in deepest Wales here. Behind, Llyn Teifi and her chriw (crew) stretch out like a necklace of pearls, and you'll eventually reach Llyn Fyrddon Fach and Llyn Fyrddon Fawr for more magical, remote lake swimming.

❼ Back at the bothy, the route returns on a track around Llyn Egnant, another dammed reservoir, where, at the far end, away from the dam, I once spent a lazy summer day picnicking and swimming while skylarks sang above. In recent times though, Welsh Water has erected signs forbidding swimming here and, having enjoyed the five swims already covered in this route you may not feel too much hardship at giving this one a miss. Finally, the route descends through the wonderfully scenic Cwm Egnant, a steep-sided valley where the halfway mark of the Cambrian Way's upland journey between Cardiff and Conwy is recognised with a sign and a bench.

DIRECTIONS

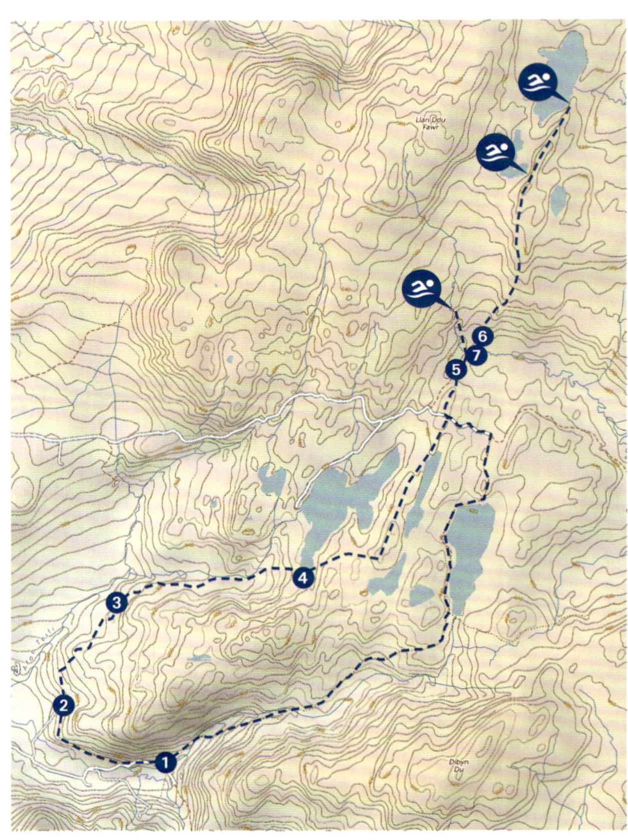

❶ From the parking area, walk down the lane in the direction of the Abbey, ignoring the first footpath on the right (this is the return route). Take the second footpath on the right, skirting the hillside below crags, through bracken which can be very overgrown. The path climbs gradually and eventually enters a field. Follow the fence line to the gate at a farmhouse.
0.7 miles

❷ Take the stony track around the right of the farm buildings and go through another gate. Follow the track uphill, then at the top turn left down towards a farmhouse and large barn. Turn right before the barn then left in front of the farmhouse and go through a gate.
0.6 miles

❸ Follow the track and branch right at the signpost. Continue uphill through Cwm Teifi, on a path that disappears into bog at times. Ignore the OS right of way on the map as this leads you straight into a bog. Instead, keep on the right of the bog on a faint track. After a mound, head left towards the fence and stream ahead. Cross a few bogs and pass a pile of stones next to the stream then veer away from the stream on a faint, dryer track uphill. Head right, below the Llyn Teifi dam.
1 mile

❹ Keep to the high ground on the right of Llyn Teifi, between Llyn Teifi and Llyn Hir, following a faint track. If you want to detour to Llyn y Gorlan descend east over rough ground, using a bearing in poor visibility. Return to the high ground, continuing north, then dropping down and go through a gate. Follow the track alongside Llyn Hir where you may want to swim.

Follow the track alongside Llyn Hir then go through another gate. At the end of the track, turn left along a tarmacked road. At the road's rise, take a faint track right leading down to Claerddu Bothy.
1.4 miles

❺ From the bothy, follow the stream north-west then north over rough and boggy ground to reach the Claerddu waterfall. Return to the bothy following the stream and retracing your steps.
0.5 miles

❻ Take the track that runs north-east from the bothy, signposted at first for the Cambrian Way. Climb up onto the high ground following the faint path. Near the top of this higher ground, veer left, slightly west of north, where the higher ground splits, with boggy ground in between, aiming for Carreg Naw Llyn on the map. This isn't very clear so you may want to use the grid reference SN 797 695 in poor weather and take a bearing towards Llyn Fyrddon Fach if you want to swim there. Return to the higher ground of Esgair Garregnawllyn for an easier route to Llyn Fyrddon Fawr for a final swim. Reverse this route to return to the bothy.

2.8 miles

❼ To continue from the bothy, retrace your steps along the path back to the tarmacked track, south-west. Turn left and walk along the tarmacked road, following it round past Llyn Egnant on the left. Walk all the way to the dam then continue on the track that travels in the same direction as the outflow, Nant Egnant. Ignore a footpath and gate branching off to the right and continue down through the valley. Turn right past the Cambrian Way bench, and cross the footbridge. The path then leads you out to the lane. Turn left and you're back at the parking area.

3.2 miles

Walk 25

DRYGARN FAWR

Get well and truly off the beaten path on this circular walk in the Cambrian Mountains, taking in two valleys with mountain streams and gorges to explore, and climb to the wild, windswept summit of Drygarn Fawr.

Abergwesyn Common lies in the upland plateau known as Elenydd, at the southern end of the Cambrian Mountains. A vast and remote land, shaped by humans through millennia, the seemingly endless expanse is resolutely carved through by bubbling streams, cascading down from the rich peatland above. This is a place to linger, to savour the feeling of big skies and solitude, to swim in peaty mountain water and marvel at those who inhabited this place in times long past.

The sleepy village of Abergwesyn has no real centre, being more a collection of farms and houses in the general locality. Where in the past the now-ruined church would have been the centre of the village, today the village hall provides a focal point and is the beginning of our walk. As there is good parking and toilets (temporarily closed at the time of writing) it is as convenient a place to set off as any. Before even leaving the car parking area you'll be welcomed by swifts and swallows swooping and red kites soaring overhead.

A quiet lane leads into meadows filled with buttercups and shady trees, surrounded by lush countryside. This is Cwm Gwesyn – the Gwesyn Valley, named for the river which tumbles through the hillside here from its source on the slopes of Drygarn Fawr, before joining with the Irfon at Abergwesyn. ❷ Our route begins by following the river upstream towards the source, gently climbing on a path through the narrowing valley becoming rockier and craggier as you ascend, oak trees giving way to hawthorns clinging to the steeper valley sides, and birch and willow lining the deepest sections of the gorge. The sound of water is ever present, and

INFORMATION

Good paths, lanes and tracks make up the bulk of the route, but there is a short, steep, grass and rock scramble and a fair amount of pathless bog-hopping to be negotiated in the middle part of the walk. You'll need good navigation skills for this route; you are likely to get your map and compass out particularly in case of poor visibility. Alternatively, the walk out and back to the waterfall is shorter and a less challenging option.

DISTANCE: 9 miles with 500m of ascent
TIME: 6 hours not including swims
MAP: OS Explorer 187 Llandovery
START & END POINT: Abergwesyn car park (SN 860 531, nearest postcode LD5 4TP)
PUBLIC TRANSPORT: Llanwrtyd Wells, five miles south, is the nearest public transport option with a train station and buses connecting to Builth Wells and Llandrindod.
SWIMMING: Mountain stream pools on the Gwesyn (SN 854 545 and SN 856 548), Sgwd y Ffrwd waterfall pool (SN 861 561) and a small gorge with pools and cascades on the Irfon (SN 842 547)
PLACES OF INTEREST: Abergwesyn Common, Drygarn Fawr summit cairns
REFRESHMENTS: Llanwrtyd is the nearest place for food, drinks and supplies. The Drovers Rest is an award-winning inn right on the river (LD5 4RA, 01591 610264). Caffi Sosban (LD5 4RB, 07407 118314) is good for hearty breakfasts and lunches.

soon the gorge becomes less steep and you will find a series of pools and cascades to dip into. It is wonderful to plunge into the deep, peaty pools while wagtails flit between the rocks and dragonflies hover by.

❸ Climbing back up after a swim here, the path snakes through the valley, contouring around the hillside until it reaches the magnificent Sgwd y Ffrwd, meaning Fall of the Stream. This multi-tiered waterfall bounces between the slabs of rock, with small pools carved out on various levels. The best pool for a refreshing swim is found by scrambling with care two-thirds of the way up the right-hand side of the falls. From here the view out over the valley is breathtaking, giving the effect of an infinity pool, albeit a very wild and cold one!

The waterfall also signals the end of the good path. From here there is a challenging section of wet, pathless and often boggy terrain to cover. An alternative to the circular route proposed in this chapter is to turn and retrace your steps from the waterfall for an out-and-back walk. ❹ Otherwise, continue on the full route, climb up above the waterfall the terrain opens out and then follow the course of the river, using sheep tracks to ease your progress where possible. In poor visibility there aren't a great many distinctive features to navigate with, so a compass bearing may be useful to ensure you're heading in the direction of Drygarn Fawr.

The bogginess may begin to feel relentless but you'll begin to understand just why these uplands play such an important role in the water cycle. As well as helping with flood prevention, healthy blanket bog locks carbon away in the vast tracts of peat. Incredibly, peatland accounts for more carbon storage globally than rainforests. However, the peatland here is not as healthy as it should be. One indicator plant species for healthy blanket bogs, Sphagnum moss, has been on the decline here since the post-industrial period, largely due to more intensive grazing practices, encouraging a rapid increase in the dominance of Molinia, also known as purple moor grass.

Peat also holds excellent records of relatively recent climate and vegetative conditions, which researchers are able to analyse using samples from the layer upon layer of preserved vegetation present in the peat. Occasionally, important archaeological finds are made, perfectly preserved in the anaerobic conditions of peat bogs. The National Trust, which owns and manages Abergwesyn Common, is working to restore the peatland here so it can maintain its important roles for future generations, following the Peatland Code for sustainable peatland management.

With a new appreciation for the bogs which you're hopping, as you climb gradually and steadily towards Drygarn Fawr, pause from time to time to catch your breath and take in the views which are revealed as you climb higher. Here the entire range of the Bannau Brycheiniog, or Brecon Beacons, National Park, stretches out in the distance, and it is possible to discern the Black Mountains in the east, the Central Beacons including the distinctive twin flat-topped peaks of Pen y Fan and Corn Du, the Fforest Fawr range, and the Mynydd Du range to the west.

Climbing higher still, boggy ground finally concedes to the rock outcrop of Drygarn Fawr's summit. Meaning Three Large Cairns, the mountain's name could not be more descriptive, save for the fact that only two large cairns survive here, separated by approximately a third of a mile. These enormous beehive cairns are spectacular and can be seen for miles around. Impressive as they are, especially when the sun glints on the quartz stones

crowning the massive structures, it is thought that they were remodelled from the original Bronze Age cairns in the 19th century.

Up here, there is a sudden, almost dizzying sense of space and remoteness and in good conditions it is well worth lingering a while, perhaps over lunch, to take it all in. If the weather is less than ideal you may want to head down to the relative shelter of the valley below. **5** Before setting off, take a compass bearing, as heading off in the wrong direction here would be inconvenient at best. More bog needs to be negotiated before you reach a blissfully solid track through the plantation forest below. The official right of way is tricky to find given the forestry tracks which have carved up the woodland, built for felling. Although not strictly the right of way, many people stick to the forestry track and hop the gate at the bottom, so this is a backup option if you struggle to locate the sometimes-overgrown footpath.

6 Emerging from the forestry into a breathtaking valley, Cwm Irfon, here a quiet road to walk on speeds your way through the valley while the screams and croaks of ravens and peregrines echo in the crags high above. A vibrant green in spring, flaming copper colours spread through the valley as the bracken rusts during autumn. The river Irfon tumbles through, burrowing a dramatic gorge known as Camddwr Bleiddiad, Wolf's Leap. This is a wonderful place to spend some time for a final swim, dipping in and out of the pools or exploring deeper into the gorge from below. Rest your bog-weary legs and dry off on the warm rocks in the afternoon sunshine before making your way back along the lane to complete the circle. It's a treat you won't forget in a long time.

DIRECTIONS

1 From the village hall, turn right along the lane, heading north-east, then turn up the track on your left. Pass the house on the left and after a short distance go through the gate into the field on your right. Walk on the track through the field until you reach the stream. Turn left and follow the fence along before crossing the stream.

0.6 miles

2 Go through the trees and veer away from the obvious track, cross the open field into the trees again, picking up another path which takes you to Trysgol farm. Follow the track from the farm north-west into Cwm Gwesyn. Just as the track descends and approaches the river on the left, go left off the track to reach the stream and find the first set of pools for a dip.

0.7 miles

3 Return to the track and continue through the valley with the stream on your left. Descend again to another set of pools a little further along, for more swimming. Return to the track once again and continue following it through the valley until you reach Sgwd Ffrwd waterfall which will be easily recognisable as it is the largest around. Circumnavigate the boggy ground and climb up to the second level of the falls to find a deep pool for another swim.

1.2 miles

4 Continue climbing up to the top of the waterfall and then follow the stream closely, keeping it on your left. In good weather you'll be able to clearly see and head for the summit of Drygarn Fawr up ahead. Otherwise, you'll need to follow a bearing from the junction of three streams at grid ref SN 859 574 across boggy ground to the cairn on Drygarn Fawr, north-north-east.

1.5 miles

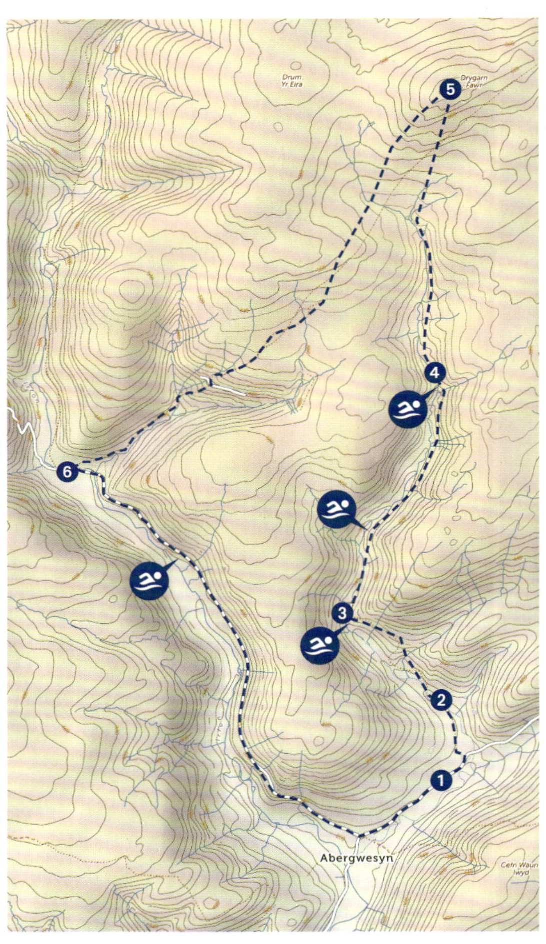

5 From the trig point, follow a more defined path south-west to a stream crossing at grid ref SN 857 576. From here take another bearing to grid ref SN 848 564 to enter the forestry area. Follow the footpath to the forest track then drop down to the next track and

take the right of way into the forest again, crossing a stream and descending with another stream below, continue behind the house and join the lane. Alternatively, if the right of way is impassable or you have difficulty finding it, when you first reach the forest track continue on this as it curves round to the left-hand side of the valley, and hop over the gate at the end. This isn't strictly speaking a right of way, so avoid it if forestry operations are in progress.
2.5 miles

❻ Turn left on the lane, following it south-east through the valley. Cut down to the river at SN 842 547 or anywhere upstream to reach the Camddwr Bleiddiad (Wolf's Leap) pools and gorge.
2.7 miles

Walk 26

DOETHIE VALLEY AND LLYN BRIANNE

A challenging walk through the remote splendour of the Doethie Valley with a mountain stream and mini gorge to explore, a deep, swirling pool where two rivers meet, lonely forest tracks and views high over the expanse of Llyn Brianne reservoir.

The Tywi flows for 75 miles from its source at Crug Gynon in the vast boggy expanse of the Elenydd uplands, vaguely between the Teifi Pools and the Clearwen Reservoir of the Elan Valley. The river is interrupted after six miles by Britain's largest dam, pooling it into an enormous reservoir named Llyn Brianne. Its name is a corruption of the name of one of the other streams which pour into it, Nant y Bryniau, meaning 'Stream amongst The Hills'.

Even those who take huge pride in their Welsh geography may look at you blankly should you ask them to pinpoint Llyn Brianne or the source of the Tywi on a map. Before a road associated with the building of Llyn Brianne's dam was constructed connecting Llanwrtyd Wells and Llandovery to the east with Tregaron to the west, it truly was in the middle of nowhere. Our walk begins from a bridge downstream from the reservoir, where the Tywi flows freely again.

Shortly after leaving the reservoir, the Tywi meets the Doethie, and the two rivers merge, swirling into a deep, cold confluence locally known as Junction Pool, the first opportunity for a swim on our route. There is something special about the energy here as you step into the bitingly cold water. Perhaps it is the dynamism of the rivers as their waters combine, or perhaps it is the iciness of the Tywi when it flows from the depths of the reservoir, mist rising from the water in the early morning as the sun hits the crag in the distance and a flash of blue catches your eye as a kingfisher darts past.

INFORMATION

A committing walk with few escape options; a good level of self-sufficiency and preparedness is advised. Quiet lanes, boggy and muddy trails, forestry tracks and a very steep climb. You can split the route over two days at the wonderful Ty'n Cornel hostel, which would involve a two-mile detour halfway through.

DISTANCE: 13½ miles, 650m ascent
TIME: 6 hours not including swims
MAP: OS Explorer 187 Llandovery
START & END POINT: Layby near Gallt y Bere bridge, a little south-west of the RSPB Gwenffrwd-Dinas reserve (SN 774 459, nearest postcode SA20 0PH)
PUBLIC TRANSPORT: Llandovery, 10 miles south, is the nearest public transport option with a train station and buses. Arrange a taxi from there or, alternatively, from Tregaron to the west, where buses are available.
SWIMMING: Large pool at the junction where the Tywi and the Doethie rivers meet (SN 777 466) – be aware of higher river levels if water is being released from the reservoir, a pool on the Doethie (SN 774 472) and a deep pool in a small gorge below a cascade on the Doethie (SN 767 499)
PLACES OF INTEREST: Twm Siôn Cati's Cave and RSPB Gwenffrwd Dinas Nature Reserve (just off route), Llyn Brianne Dam (just off route), Soar y Mynydd chapel (just off route)
REFRESHMENTS: The Towy Bridge Inn (SA20 0PE, 01550 760370) is on the banks of the Tywi near Rhandirmwyn with plentiful home-cooked food. Y Talbot (SY25 6JL, 01974 298208) in Tregaron is excellent.

Or maybe it is in the ancient woodland that covers the slopes of the steep-sided hill at Gwenffrwd Dinas on the opposite bank, reputed to have once been the refuge of renowned outlaw Twm Siôn Cati, who hid out in a cave on the slopes just above the pool whilst attempting to woo a wealthy widow from nearby Ystradffin Farm. Thomas Jones, as Twm was properly known, is a legendary Welsh figure born in Tregaron in the 1500s. Legend has him penned as a common outlaw, a Welsh Robin Hood whom history holds responsible for more misdeeds and trickery than can possibly have been done by one man. What is known about him is that he was an illegitimate son descending from Welsh nobility and was an accomplished bard and poet. He was a staunch Protestant which gave him the status of a rebel at a time when refusing to practice Mary I's Catholicism could get you killed, and he no doubt had to hustle to survive. After his death, Twm's exploits became legendary and his cave became a draw for 19th century tourists.

The same hill and woodland, Gwenffrwd Dinas, where he hid out, is an RSPB reserve, designated when red kites were still scarce in Wales and this part of the upper Tywi was one of their last refuges. The reserve is not accessible from this side of the river, but if you have time before or after the walk to visit from the entrance on the other side, you can still find Twm's cave tucked away in the hillside. The woodland surrounding Junction Pool is Celtic Rainforest, a rare pocket in an otherwise tree denuded landscape. This type of Atlantic Temperate Rainforest thrives in the steep sided gorge and hillside of the reserve. Swimming in this deep, dark, swirling pool with a damp, leafy scent filling the air, the sound of water cascading around and light glittering through the trees is utterly spellbinding. A visit during spring will surround you in mesmerising bird song, and in autumn the turning colours form a soothing spectrum in the canopy.

❷ Climbing back up from the pool, we continue on the quiet lane which follows the Doethie upstream, to another tempting spot to enjoy a river dip, just off the verge, where a gentle gravel beach slopes into the water. After passing through a farm at the road's end, our route swings north into the Doethie Valley, a favourite walking route for connoisseurs of off-the-beaten-path places in Wales. ❸ We join the Cambrian Way long distance walking route which traverses the uplands of Wales from Cardiff to Conwy, as it passes through the valley. The landscape here is a site to behold and changes throughout the year. It's equally lovely when the cuckoos are calling and woodpeckers pecking in

spring, when the hillsides are bursting into vibrant green and heads of white flowers froth on the trees, or in autumn when the bracken and heather rusts to turn the slopes of the valley to bronze, the river snakes through and kites soar overhead.

After a while, just before the path bends around the craggy slope, the valley narrows with a deep gorge. If you're willing to negotiate the boggy and tussocky slope (delicate ankles beware!) then you can get into the river and paddle upstream on foot to the bottom of the gorge. There you'll find a very deep pool below a set of cascades, overhung by rowan trees and hidden from the world above. This is a real adventure and will be easier or more challenging depending on the river levels with recent rainfall; if the river is flowing particularly high and fast it may not be possible to get in at all, let alone paddle upstream. Wearing something to protect your feet will be advantageous, and ensuring a safe exit is key before you get in; you are a long way from help here so use careful judgement. Getting changed will be a huge source of entertainment as you try to balance between tufts of grass.

❹ Continuing along the valley it widens again then you'll find yourself in a pocket of trees with a stream babbling through. Nearby, a waterfall sounds from beyond the trees and, although still on open access land, you'll be hard pressed to reach

it, with barbed wire fences surrounding the steep gorge it has created. A shame, as there is a perfect pool at the bottom.

Although the route turns up from the Doethie valley here, a couple of miles further along is Ty'n Cornel hostel, one of the Elenydd Wilderness Hostels. If you want to extend your time out here and experience hostelling as it used to be, far from the nearest tarmacked road and in one of the best dark sky locations in Wales, I highly recommend detouring and spending the night, splitting this route over two days.

❺ A steep, relentless climb awaits but a reward comes in the form of exceptional views back down the valley. Clear felling of the plantation forestry has blotted the landscape in recent years but this will fade and soften in years to come. ❻ A pleasant walk through enclosed farmland comes next; those with a keen eye will be able to spot the apex of Drygarn Fawr (Walk 25) directly ahead and perhaps even its huge beehive summit cairn.

As you reach the farm and descend to the forestry track junction, the north-western arm of Llyn Brianne comes into view. A little way north of here is the iconic Soar y Mynydd chapel; a Calvinist Methodist chapel known to be the most remote in Wales. Built in 1822, the chapel served the sparse population of farmers long before the forestry plantations, dams and roads arrived. It is a worthwhile detour for its reverent atmosphere if you have additional miles in your legs.

❼ Continuing on the route, the forestry track beckons. If forestry operations are taking place, you may find a detour here, but otherwise stick to the main track and you'll get an insight into the vast forestry industry that plays such a prominent part in the Welsh landscape. Clear felling is controversial at best, and the areas where this has been done are truly stark, as though a brutal apocalypse or natural disaster has taken place. It is a striking contrast to the pockets of rainforest and you can't help thinking that there must be a better way, especially when you see the rivers running brown as the exposed peaty soil is washed from the hillsides after each heavy rainfall.

Soon, views open up over the reservoir and it really does make for a beautiful scene. The view before the dam was constructed and the valley flooded just sixty years ago would have been vastly different. Although there was local opposition at the time, particularly from villagers downriver at Rhandirmwyn, who were concerned about a catastrophic dam failure, construction went ahead and was completed in the 1970s. In the early 2000s, Welsh Water secured a bylaw preventing any recreational access to the reservoir, other than for fee-paying anglers. This was partly in response to death-defying kayakers paddling down the spillway, reaching speeds of up to 45 miles per hour! Unfortunately, the blanket recreation ban includes all watercraft, swimmers and bathers.

❽ Leaving the reservoir behind you, a pleasant descent closes the loop back at Troed-rhiw Cymmer farm, from where you'll retrace your earlier steps to return to the start.

DIRECTIONS

❶ Begin at the Gallt y Bere bridge over the Tywi, crossing it northwards and turning right. Follow the lane along until you reach a dwelling on the left, and a small outcrop of rock on your right. Just beyond this outcrop, on the right, is a path leading through the trees, descending gently at first before it narrows and descends steeply to a pool where the two rivers meet, for a first swim.
0.8 miles

❷ Return to the lane and turn right, following it with the river on your right then, as you cross the bridge, it'll be on your left. Soon after the bridge there is a small gravel beach on your left leading to a deeper section of the river where another swim is possible. Continue on the road to the farm Troed-rhiw-ruddwen. Turn left to go through the farmyard and go through the gate to continue on the track above the farm buildings. Walk down the track until you see a path off to the right, signposted for the Cambrian Way.
1.4 miles

❸ Follow the path onto the hillside and follow it north-west and then north as it contours along the east side of the valley, with the river below to your left. As a crag appears ahead and the valley narrows, drop down over tussocky, boggy ground to reach the river before the rocky, tree-lined gorge. If river levels allow, it is possible to get in the water here and paddle up with care to reach a deep pool below a small cascade for a final swim.
1.3 miles

❹ Return to the path and continue north, as you round the crag above the gorge and the valley widens again. Follow the path all the way into trees and go through two gates, hop a stream then turn west until you see a path heading off uphill to the east, signposted as a bridleway. Note that the rights of way on the OS map are not accurately reflected on the ground here. After a short section which can get overgrown with bracken, you'll pop out onto a clearer path; cross above the footings of an old stone dwelling, and climb alongside the narrow stream to your right.
1.2 miles

❺ Cross the stream at the top and turn left, uphill, and go through a gate. Continue steeply uphill following the fence line until a clearer track appears and swings left, then right, climbing more gently. At the top, the track reaches a gate.
0.4 miles

❻ Go through the gate and continue on the track through another gate. Walk on the track downhill until you reach a farmhouse. Turn right to go in front of the farmhouse then straight ahead on the main track. Follow this downhill until you reach the forestry track on the right.
1 mile

❼ Turn right and walk along the forestry track. Go through the barrier and continue until there is a choice of two tracks. Turn left. At the next junction, ignore the left turning and continue ahead. Keep to the lower path as it curves around above the valley, ignoring an uphill track on the right. You'll then pass a minor track on your left leading down into the trees; ignore this and continue above a house on your left.
3.7 miles

❽ Stick to the main track, ignoring another major track heading up to the right, and finally you'll reach a cattle grid. Go over the cattle grid then take the track on the right-hand side. This leads down through a valley back to Troed-rhiw-ruddwen farm. Turn left at the bottom of the track to return to the lane.
2 miles

❾ Follow the lane all the way back to the Gallt y Bere bridge.
1.9 miles

Walk 27

ABERGORLECH

Walk through the Gorlech Valley on forestry tracks, with small pools for dipping along the river. Then return to the village and the River Cothi for an adventurous swim in a deep section of gorge.

Abergorlech, the pretty village which this walk centres on, is found in the depths of the Carmarthenshire countryside. It lies in the lush green Cothi valley, a few miles west of Talley and its abbey ruins, founded in the 12th century by Lord Rhys, ruler of the southern Wales Kingdom of Deuheubarth. No matter from which direction you arrive, it is clear how the surrounding countryside idyll could give rise to great poets: prophetic poet Dafydd Gorlech who performed for nobility, and Lewis Glyn Cothi from nearby Rhydycymerau, both influential bards of the 1400s with political and royal connections, came from here. Lewis Glyn Cothi took his bardic name from the area, and much of his poetry protested the oppression of the Welsh since the Owain Glyndwr uprising in the 15th century.

The minor road which runs through the centre of the village is lined with whitewashed cottages, rose and vegetable gardens, and a traditional pub. A sign displaying its dominance in Best-Kept Village competitions throughout the 1960s is still proudly on display.

The walk begins at the Abergorlech forestry car park. It explores part of the sprawling Brechfa Forest, managed by Natural Resources Wales and recently enveloped as part of the National Forest for Wales, a Welsh Government project to create a network of connected forests across Wales. Brechfa has long been renowned for its woodland. It was once a Royal Forest, an area set aside by Norman kings for hunting by them and other members of the aristocracy. Commoners, everyday folk, were excluded from it by Forest Law, in order to prevent damage to vegetation, and to protect certain game wildlife such as deer, boar and wolf. Breaking Forest

INFORMATION

Mixed terrain: forestry tracks, some narrow woodland paths which can be muddy, a small section of lane walking and riverside meadow and woodland, boggy in places.

DISTANCE: 4 miles
TIME: 2 hours not including swims
MAP: OS Explorer 186 Llandeilo & Brechfa Forest
START & END POINT: Abergorlech Forestry car park (SN 586 337, SA32 7SL)
PUBLIC TRANSPORT: Bus 283 between Llandeilo and Carmarthen stops at the Black Lion in Abergorlech, near the start of the route, once each direction, Wednesdays and Saturdays only.
SWIMMING: Shallow pool for dipping (SN 585 341), a deeper pool (SN 575 357) and a deep, flowing gorge (SN 588 335)
PLACES OF INTEREST: Forest Garden (just off route), Pont Cothi ancient bridge
REFRESHMENTS: Y Llew Du / Black Lion, Abergorlech has a generous menu of delicious, freshly cooked food, with cosy traditional bar, restaurant, and outside garden overlooking the river (SA32 7SL, 01558 685271).

Law carried harsh punishments. This did allow a certain protection for the ancient woodland here; once Forest Law ceased to be in force, the ancient forest was cleared. It had all but gone by the 17th century when the forest was exploited for wood tar. Oak saplings were used for oil and alder was used for charcoal and in making gunpowder during the First World War. Following the war, state plantation forest was established here at Brechfa, with quick-growing, non-native tree species planted to contribute to the national stock of timber.

In the 1920s a labour camp, one of 25 established in Britain to address high levels of unemployment, was set up in Brechfa. It wasn't compulsory for unemployed men to attend but they had little choice as their social security payments depended on them doing so. The men in the camps built the forestry roads and turned the farms into timber plantations. The camp was also briefly used to house refugee boys from Guernica during the Spanish civil war.

Setting off from the forestry car park the route follows the Gorlech river upstream, through fern and moss-carpeted woodland, across well-made footbridges with small dipping pools underneath. The water is supremely clear and reflects the lush mixed canopy above. This section of woodland is mainly deciduous; the forest beyond is mixed plantation. There are options for extending the walk to visit the Forest Garden, where a variety of trees from around the world were once planted to see which would grow best here, including giant Californian redwoods, Australian eucalyptus and a range of firs.

The route begins gently, alongside the river, then climbs more steeply. If you're lucky on a sunny day you may come across an adder basking on the warm gravel of the forest track, and see red kites and buzzards wheeling overhead. Keep a lookout for the famous Gorlech Stones, which have

been found in the river here. The stones are round, approximately football-sized, and have unique patterns. Known in geological terms as septarian nodules, the rocks are formed from mudstone that has dried, forming cracks which were later replaced by calcite. The river erodes the mudstone away, leaving the harder calcite, forming strange and beautiful shapes. If you're not lucky enough to find one in the river, have a look in the gardens in the village when you're next passing; some of the residents have the stones on display. The most alluring swim spot is found at the top of the track, where it bends and crosses the river. The trees open up here, allowing the sun to reach the water, inviting you in to the deep pool directly below the track, framed by alders, willows and ferns.

Return downstream on the other side of the river, high on the forested banks where the plantation fir trees transport you to an entirely different environment, one of pine needles soft underfoot, and of goldcrests singing loudly in the trees above.

The smallest bird in Wales, Britain and indeed Europe, it nevertheless has a song which pierces through the valley in a high trill, and a flash of gold on its head makes it a delight to come across. Once you've learnt its distinctive call you won't forget it.

Returning to the centre of the village on a track, you'll come out conveniently close to Y Llew Du (The Black Lion) pub. A traditional pub with a cosy bar and fire area inside for the colder days, and a riverside beer garden outside overlooking the ancient Pont Cothi bridge, this is the perfect pitstop to rest and refuel before heading off for a final swim.

Walking through the village along the main road which returns to the forest car park entrance, you'll again cross the Gorlech as it careers down to meet the Cothi. The name of the village, Abergorlech represents this meeting of the two rivers. A narrow and often muddy footpath enters a meadow then turns into the woodland towards the River Cothi. As the path meets the riverbank there is a section of deep, steep-sided gorge, banked by mossy covered rocks and shaded by a canopy of oak. The Cothi is a river to be revered. It's a tributary of the Tywi, which it meets near Carmarthen. Long known for its population of salmon, sewin (sea trout) and brown trout, the river has a long fishing heritage. There are fishing rights all along the river here and it is important to respect any anglers who might be present.

A swim here is committing; it is possible to enter the water from the rocks and shallows at the top end of the gorge, but once in there is no feasible way out of the water downstream without scrambling about on the delicate mossy banks – to be avoided. Before entering, assess the depth of the flow and make sure you can swim back upstream against it to exit where you've entered. Be aware that the deep water can be numbingly cold and hold a strong current even when it looks calm and inviting on the surface; approach tentatively and with caution.

That all taken into account, in calm summer conditions this is one of the most magical inland spots to swim, transported to a world of shimmering gold-green above water, and copper-emerald below. Strong swimmers can enjoy floating down on the current and swimming back against it. Bring your goggles and look for fish below the surface; sit still on the bank and spot dippers and kingfishers.

DIRECTIONS

❶ From Abergorlech Forestry car park (SA32 7SL) take the track heading uphill. Look out for a footbridge on the left over the river where there is a dipping pool. Cross the bridge to walk upstream with the river now on your right. You'll soon come to another footbridge on your right with another shallow dipping pool underneath; cross that to join the forestry track on the other side.
0.5 miles

❷ Follow the forestry track uphill with the river now below you to your left. Continue on the track, ignoring a minor turn-off left to a ford, until you reach a clear branch in the track, where it crosses the river. Here is the final and deepest pool for a dip, just below the track.
1.2 miles

❸ Cross the river heading uphill and look for a path into the forest on your left. Take the path which climbs high above the river. Ignore a path zigzagging back down towards the river, but continue on until you meet a track with fields and a farm to your right. Continue down on the track as it curves to the right and emerges into the village between some houses.
1.7 miles

❹ Once out on the main road through the village, turn right to head to the pub, or turn left, crossing the Gorlech river and the forestry car park entrance. Look then for a public footpath on the right-hand side of the road, down a grassy track and into trees until it meets the Cothi river. Where the path comes alongside the river is the small section of gorge, the final swimming option.
0.2 miles

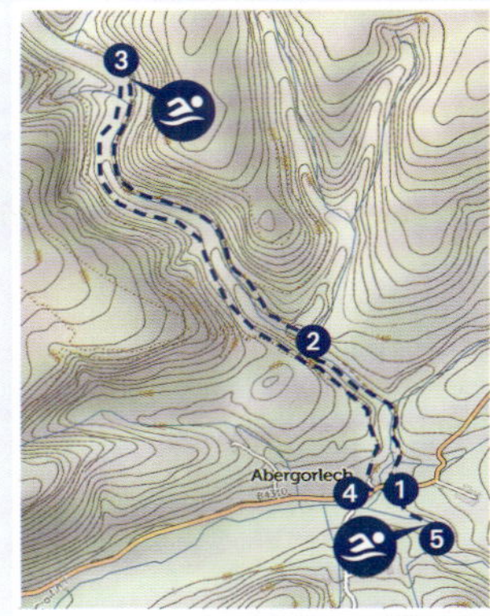

❺ Return along the footpath to the road, turn left and find the forestry car park on your right.
0.2 miles

Walk 28

HENLLAN

A short but sweet walk taking in the banks of the Teifi, a stunning set of rocky rapids and a deep gorge before an enjoyable climb through quiet woodlands and marshy farmland.

INFORMATION

The terrain can be muddy, wet and rough in places. There are two short sections of lane walking. In both cases, you will need to judge the water conditions carefully. The Teifi suffers from pollution particularly after rain, so check the river app.

DISTANCE: 3 miles
TIME: 1½ hours excluding swims
MAP: OS Explorer 185 Newcastle Emlyn
START & END POINT: Bus stop in Henllan village (SN 359 406, SA44 5TJ). Park considerately in the village, near the bridge, or head out on the small lane to grid ref SN 366 406 for pull-ins to park.
PUBLIC TRANSPORT: Bus 460 from Carmarthen to Newcastle Emlyn stops at Henllan. Carmarthen enjoys good train connections.
SWIMMING: Deep pool in the Teifi (SN 361 403) and a deep section of gorge below the bridge (SN 356 401)
PLACES OF INTEREST: Henllan bridge, Teifi Valley Railway, Henllan Bridge prisoner of war camp, National wool museum (½ mile from Henllan), Cenarth falls and mill, and the National Coracle Centre (all 6 miles from Henllan)
REFRESHMENTS: The Leeky Barrel (SA44 5TD, 01559 372 152) is a fantastic log cabin style café where you'll be able to try all the Welsh classic. Slightly further afield, the Daffodil Inn (SA44 5NG, 01559 370343) in Penrhiw-llan is an excellent Michelin-listed pub with delicious brunches, Sunday roasts and vegan options.

Having visited the Teifi at its source (Walk 24), and near its mouth (Walk 15), it is only fitting to visit the longest river in West Wales in the middle of its journey to the sea, an opportunity to gain a fuller understanding of its nature and heritage. A few miles upstream from Henllan, the river bounces between rocks and foams into white water, much to the delight of paddlesport enthusiasts who enjoy kayaking and rafting through the rapids. The paddlesport centre there also offers guided river swimming, should you want some hands-on guidance to enjoy the river safely. Downstream, at the village of Cenarth, a set of falls and salmon leaps has been a long-standing visitor attraction. There, an 18th century corn mill replaced one dating back to the 13th century. You can also visit the National Coracle Centre (coracles are the primitive type of boats once used widely in this area) to learn more about how humans have been interacting with the river for centuries.

In Henllan itself, the village you see today is a relatively modern settlement, though there is an interesting past here with much to discover. The route begins by walking the short distance from the village to the adjoining hamlet of Trebedw, meeting a path leading down towards the river. If you are parking elsewhere, you can easily make your way to join the walk at this point.

❷ There are strict instructions, via a sign, to stick to a path in the middle of the field which borders the river; this feels frustrating but you'll be at the river in no time. The path takes you into trees below a very steep bank, above which the main village sits. Before long, you will come across a huge pool in the river, significant enough to be given a name, Llyn y Badell – translating unpoetically as Pan or Bowl Lake, or something to that effect. Indeed, one could see this section of the river as a giant fish bowl; watch for a while and you'll see the ripples of larger fish swimming in the deep, and fry and fingerlings flitting around the edges. There is a beautiful view upstream of the wide tree-lined channel; the pool here is overhung with oak and willow. The water quickly becomes very deep, and can be fast flowing in the middle. Downstream the river becomes shallower and gathers pace towards the rapids, so swimming upstream is the better option. There are fishing rights on the river and, to avoid any conflict, treat anglers respectfully, perhaps giving this spot a miss if there is anyone fishing during your visit.

❸ Continuing on, the walk alongside the river as it sparkles below the shimmering leaves of the beech trees will make you want to linger. High on the bank above is the site which once held a prehistoric promontory fort, dating to the Iron Age. Early excavations of the area revealed the remains of roundhouses and other archaeological remnants. The site was largely built over for the construction of a Prisoner of War camp here in the 1940s. The camp housed more than a thousand Italian prisoners who had been captured in Libya and Tunisia. Later, German prisoners of war were also held here. The site was extensive, and the prisoners worked in local farms. Henllan is notable for having the only church in Britain decorated by prisoners of war; the Italianate chapel still stands to this day. Visits are possible but have to be booked in advance as the camp land is privately owned by a local family.

There were two woollen mills recorded in the village, but the main centre of activity for spinning and weaving was just a short distance down the road at Drefach Felindre. During the 1920s more than 50 mills in the area produced huge quantities of flannel used for clothing, a real hive of industry. Today the National Wool Museum housed in a huge former mill gives visitors an insight into what the wool industry meant to the area. It is less than a mile from the route so you could take a detour if you wanted to pay it a visit.

Emerging from the trees you'll come across the falls. Here the water rushes through mossy rocks, and the fir trees on the far side of the bank give this spot an almost Alpine feel. In autumn, this is as good a spot as the much more frequented Cenarth to spot fish migrating. If you're lucky enough you might be able to see the silvery and speckled salmon and trout leaping up the falls, heading upstream to spawn.

A short way down from the falls, the river falls silent as it flows through a deep, cold gorge and below the twin-arched stone bridge which is a listed monument. This is a breathtakingly beautiful spot and one in which you could easily imagine coming across the Gwragedd Annwn, 'wives of the Otherworld' who, according to local folklore were beautiful female fairies who inhabited rivers and lakes. If you want to swim here, make a good assessment of the water flow and your ability to get in and out safely. There is no access to the river downstream so you will need to get out the same way you get in. Although a road runs alongside the river and over the bridge, once down in the water this is easily forgotten, the enchanting magic of the deep, cold water reflecting the green canopy above and swirling through the smooth rocks of the gorge.

❹ Leaving the river Teifi behind now, a short section of road takes you to a pathway behind the church, now a private dwelling. The sewage works beyond is a reminder of the pressures put on the river nowadays. The walk continues on a very quiet route through woodland and under a

rail bridge. Today the only trains running here are the narrow-gauge Teifi Valley tourist trains which depart from Henllan. In its heyday in the 1890s, the line ran from Carmarthen to the east, and to Newcastle Emlyn to the west. Passenger trains stopped running in the 1950s and freight trains in the 1970s; the line was first restored and used as a leisure service in the 1980s.

(5, 6) Climbing steadily up to a path along the side of the Afon Cynllo, the gorge is surprisingly impressive: thickly vegetated, steep-sided banks drop precipitously to the river roaring out of sight far below. Reminiscent of a walk through Waterfall Country in the Bannau Brycheiniog (Brecon Beacons) or the Celtic rainforests of Eryri (Snowdonia), this thoroughly enjoyable section of the route is over all too soon. 7 A brief interlude of lane walking leads you into pleasant, marshy fields where sheep graze and only a family of noisy jays may interrupt the tranquillity. An enormous oak tree stands tall with a full crown of leaves, standing strong despite being completely hollowed out, a sign of its antiquity. 8 Crossing the railway line again, a number of fairy houses mark the terminus of the Teifi Valley Railway's 'Fairy Line', a miniature railway for visiting families.

Dropping back down to the village, brambles, gorse and bracken offer a late summer embrace, leaving their mark in your hair and clothes, but the delicious blackberries more than make up for it. Should you be visiting out of season, console yourself with a visit to the wonderful Leeky Barrel café for post-walk sustenance and to get a real flavour of the region. This is also home to the wonderful Celteg Wines company, who create fruit wines, mead, liqueur and any number of jams and chutneys, with many ingredients foraged from the surrounding countryside or grown on site.

DIRECTIONS

1 From the bus stop, walk east through the village towards the Trebedw side. Go down the hill and take a turning on the right. Before a house on the right, look for the path on the right with railings separating it from the garden. Turn right at the bottom to go on a track and through a gate into the field.
0.4 miles

2 Walk through the middle of the meadow, then cross the footbridge and turn left. Walk alongside the river to a large pool on your left, for a first swim.
0.3 miles

3 Follow the path alongside the river to the bridge. Small narrow trails lead off towards the river to the falls, and then to the gorge below the bridge for another opportunity to swim carefully.
0.4 miles

4 Return to the path and join the road, heading uphill away from the bridge. Turn left down the track and walk behind the church. Follow the path past the sewage works and into the wood.
0.3 miles

5 Continue following signs through the trees then turn left onto a track, followed by a right through a gate. Go under a rail bridge and continue on the path above the gorge until you reach a house / farm.
0.6 miles

6 Before the house / farm, turn right through a gate then left through another gate into a field. Continue through the field on the left-hand side, past a drive and don't turn up the track going through the middle of the field. Instead keep on the left and go down to the corner where there is a gate, somewhat hidden, in the hedge in the corner. Cross a footbridge and come out onto a track, then turn right to meet the lane.
0.2 miles

7 Turn right, uphill past a house on the right, then take a left onto the lane signed 'Llangrannog 10 miles'. Take a track on the right. Go through the gate and through the fields past a derelict house and large hollowed out oak tree. Take a right along a hedgerow to a gate. Go through the gate then turn left and cross the field to a small gate.
0.4 miles

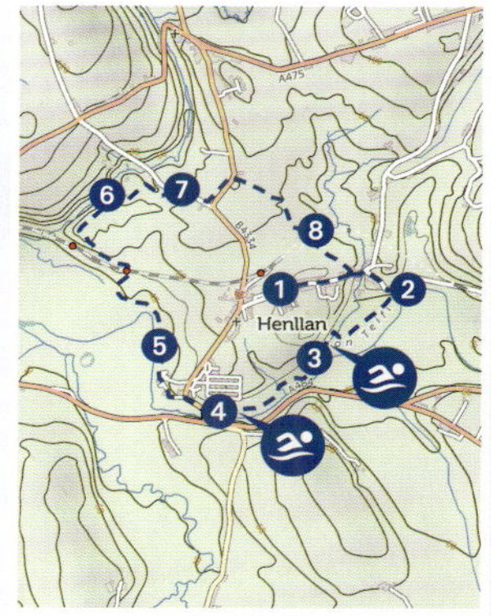

8 Go over the bridge next to the miniature railway, then turn left before a gate to go through trees along an overgrown pathway. Continue downhill, and walk through the gate onto the driveway outside a house. Join the road and turn right to arrive back in the centre of the village at the bus stop.
0.4 miles

Health, Safety and Responsibility. Like any water-based activity wild swimming has risks and can be dangerous and these are described more fully inside. None of the locations featured in this book have lifeguards and all could include risks such as as strong currents, cold water, occasional pollution, slips, trips and falls etc. The author and publisher have gone to great lengths to ensure the accuracy of the information herein but cannot be held legally or financially responsible for accident, injury, loss or inconvenience sustained as a result of the information or advice contained. Swimming, jumping, diving, scrambling or any other activities is entirely at your own risk.

Acknowledgements

Huge thanks once again to all at Wild Things Publishing for giving me the opportunity to work on this dream project. Special mention to my editor, Michael Lee; it was a privilege to work with you for a second time. I'm grateful for your meticulous eye and enthusiasm. Thanks to Amy Bolt for making it all look so beautiful and James Lewis for the stunning cover artwork. Thank you to my family - Andrew, Lila, Amber, Sunny and Clara and Mum - for memories that I'll cherish forever, and for your support during the many days I was away exploring, or writing at the desk. To the many wonderful, adventurous friends who joined me to try the walks, to be models, and often to lend moral support, this book would not have happened without you. Nia, Emma, Deb, Holly M, Ady, Jo, Aisha, Alex, Rachael, Mari, Nicola, Lou, Lucy, Holly G, Grace and the Walk the Edges ladies, you are all more wonderful than you know!

Photo credits

All photos by Nia Lloyd Knott except page 116 (Emma Hayhurst) and page 194 bottom (Mari Owen)

Editor:
Michael Lee
Cover illustration:
James Lewis
Design and layout:
Amy Bolt
Proofreading:
Tania Pascoe
Mapping powered by:

Published by:
Wild Things Publishing Ltd
Bath, BA2 7WG,
United Kingdom
wildthingspublishing.com

Other books from Wild Things Publishing:

Snorkelling Britain
Wild Guide West Ireland
Wild Guide North East
Wild Guide Wales
Wild Guide Scotland
Wild Guide Central England
Wild Guide Lakes & Dales
Wild Guide South-West
Wild Guide London South-East
Wild Guide Isle of Man
Wild Guide Morocco
Wild Guide Scandinavia
Wild Guide Portugal
Wild Guide French Alps
Wild Guide Greece
Wild Guide Andalucia
Wild Guide Balearic Islands
Wild Swimming Walks Yorkshire
Wild Swimming Walks West Wales
Wild Swimming Walks Bristol & Bath
Wild Swimming Walks Cornwall
Wild Swimming Walks Dorset
Wild Swimming Walks Dartmoor
Wild Swimming Walks Exmoor
Wild Swimming Walks London
Wild Swimming Walks South Wales
Wild Swimming Walks Snowdonia
Wild Swimming Walks London
Wild Swimming Walks Lake District
Wild Swimming Walks Peak District
Wild Swimming Britain
Wild Swimming France
Wild Swimming Italy
Wild Swimming Spain
Wild Swimming Alps
Wild Swimming Croatia & Slovenia
Wild Fishing Britain
Wild Saunas Britain
Paddle Boarding South East
Paddle Boarding South West
Paddle Boarding Wales
Outdoor Swimming London
Hidden Beaches Britain / Spain
Lost Lanes South
Lost Lanes Wales
Lost Lanes West
Lost Lanes North
Lost Lanes Central
Bikepacking / France en Velo
Magical Britain / France
Wild Running Britain
Wild Ruins / Ruins B.C.
Wild Garden Weekends
Scottish Bothy Bible / Walks